Cross-cultural Knowledge Management

Knowledge has become increasingly complex and important for organizations. Despite the growing recognition of the factors that enable knowledge management in organizations, our understanding about the unique cross-cultural challenges is rather limited. In particular, how cultural differences influence people's participation in knowledge management activities still remains unclear.

By conducting qualitative case studies and analytic hierarchical process (AHP) with multinational firms in Brazil and China, this book addresses the broader issue of cultural influences on knowledge management. Specific emphasis has been put on their indigenous cultural norms, including *guanxi*, *face* and *jeitinho* and the impacts they have on knowledge sharing. Drawing on an integrative knowledge management model, the results from AHP analysis reveal how some cultural-specific factors related to people, process and knowledge can affect the effectiveness of socialization, externalization and internalization processes in a production context.

The book will be useful to both management academics and business practitioners. While academics will gain insight into the intricacies of knowledge sharing activities in production organizations, managers will find some useful conceptual tools to resolve the challenges of knowledge management in a cross-cultural context.

Jacky Hong is Professor of Management at the University of Macau. He received his PhD from Lancaster University. His research interests fall into the areas of organizational learning and knowledge management with publications in *Journal of Management Studies*, *Organization Studies* and others.

Jorge Muniz Jr. is Professor of Operations Management at the Sao Paulo State University. He received his PhD from University of Sao Paulo. His research interests fall into the areas of organizational and knowledge management with publications in *Journal of Knowledge Management* and others.

Routledge Advances in Management and Business Studies

Family Business and Management
Objectives, Theory, and Practice
Magdalena Biel and Beata Ślusarczyk

Consumer Packaging Strategy
Localisation in Asian Markets
Huda Khan, Richard Lee and Polymeros Chrysochou

Distress Risk and Corporate Failure Modelling
The State of the Art
Stewart Jones

Collaborative Leadership and Innovation
Management, Strategy and Creativity
Elis Carlström

Crowdsourcing for Innovation in Higher Education
Regina Lenart-Gansiniec and Łukasz Sułkowski

The Corporation of the Future
Edited by Stuart Orr and Paul Hunter

Organizational Management and the COVID-19 Crisis
Security and Risk Management Dilemmas
Edited by Wioletta Sylwia Wereda, Jacek Woźniak and Justyna Stochaj

Digital Entrepreneurship and the Global Economy
Edited by J. Mark Munoz

Cross-cultural Knowledge Management
Cultural Influences in China and Brazil
Jacky Hong and Jorge Muniz Jr.

For more information about this series, please visit: www.routledge.com/Routledge-Advances-in-Management-and-Business-Studies/book-series/SE0305

Cross-cultural Knowledge Management

Cultural Influences in China and Brazil

Jacky Hong and Jorge Muniz Jr.

Routledge
Taylor & Francis Group
LONDON AND NEW YORK

First published 2023
by Routledge
4 Park Square, Milton Park, Abingdon, Oxon OX14 4RN

and by Routledge
605 Third Avenue, New York, NY 10158

Routledge is an imprint of the Taylor & Francis Group, an informa business

British Library Cataloguing-in-Publication Data
A catalogue record for this book is available from the British Library

Library of Congress Cataloging-in-Publication Data
Names: Hong, Jacky, author. | Muniz, Jorge, Jr., author.
Title: Cross-cultural knowledge management: cultural influences in China and Brazil/Jacky Hong and Jorge Muniz Jr.
Description: Milton Park, Abingdon, Oxon; New York, NY: Routledge, 2023. | Series: Routledge advances in management and business studies | Includes bibliographical references and index. | Identifiers: LCCN 2022029187 (print) | LCCN 2022029188 (ebook) | ISBN 9780367630959 (hardback) | ISBN 9780367630997 (paperback) | ISBN 9781003112136 (ebook)
Subjects: LCSH: Knowledge management—China—Cross-cultural studies. | Knowledge management—Brazil—Cross-cultural studies.
Classification: LCC HD30.2. H6618 2023 (print) | LCC HD30.2 (ebook) | DDC 658.4/038—dc23/eng/20220705
LC record available at https://lccn.loc.gov/2022029187
LC ebook record available at https://lccn.loc.gov/2022029188

ISBN: 978-0-367-63095-9 (hbk)
ISBN: 978-0-367-63099-7 (pbk)
ISBN: 978-1-003-11213-6 (ebk)

DOI: 10.4324/9781003112136

Typeset in Galliard
by KnowledgeWorks Global Ltd.

Contents

List of Figures vi
List of Tables vii
Preface viii
Acknowledgements xi
Acronyms xii

1 **Introduction** 1
JACKY HONG AND JORGE MUNIZ Jr.

2 **Cross-cultural Knowledge Management: Issues and Challenges** 20
JACKY HONG AND JORGE MUNIZ Jr.

3 **Managing Knowledge in China and Brazil** 41
JACKY HONG AND JORGE MUNIZ Jr.

4 **Comparative Case Studies** 58
JACKY HONG, JORGE MUNIZ Jr., ADILSON A. M. COSTILHAS, MARIANA B. SIMÕES, ALESSANDRO J. SACHO & FÁBIO K. NAKANISHI

5 **Cross-cultural Analysis of Knowledge Sharing in China and Brazil** 81
JACKY HONG, JORGE MUNIZ Jr., ADILSON A. M. COSTILHAS & MARIANA B. SIMÕES

6 **Concluding Remarks** 104
JACKY HONG AND JORGE MUNIZ Jr.

Appendices 115
Index 134

Figures

1.1 Net inflows of foreign direct investment in Brazil and China from 2002 to 2019 2

1.2 Employment in key industries in Brazil and China from 2002 to 2019 (% of total employment) 14

2.1 Knowledge management and its paradigms 21

2.2 Knowledge-based integrated production management model 27

4.1 Vertical Kaplan turbine and synchronous electrical generator unit 59

5.1 Hierarchical factors supporting knowledge sharing among production workers 84

5.2 Sample question of pairwise comparison of factors 85

Tables

1.1 Statistics on China's OFDI from 2002 to 2019 (unit: US$100 million) 2
1.2 Top 20 countries/regions with China's OFDIs in 2018 (unit: US$100 million) 3
1.3 China's utilization of foreign capital (IFDI) from 2000 to 2019 4
1.4 China's foreign direct investment in Portuguese-speaking countries (US$ million) 5
1.5 Statistics on Brazil's OFDI from 2002 to 2019 (unit: US$100 million) 7
1.6 Sectoral distribution of main BMN groups and the exporting companies 7
1.7 Statistics on Brazil's IFDI from 2002 to 2020 (unit: US$100 million) 8
1.8 Comparison between FDI inflows and outflows in Brazil and China (unit: US$100 million) 10
1.9 Top five companies in Brazil and China (US$ billion) 12
1.10 Opportunities and challenges in Brazil and China 13
2.1 Varieties of knowing in action 23
2.2 Different perspectives and characteristics of knowledge 24
2.3 Process factors 28
5.1 IPC-AHP respondents by plants 84
5.2 Example of incomplete pairwise comparison 85
5.3 Profile of interviewees 86
5.4 AHP data summary (Maxion) 87
5.5 AHP data summary (GE Hydro) 95
6.1 Industry 4.0 technologies and skills requirements 106
6.2 Soft skills required for Industry 4.0 109
A1 Managers interviewed 116
A2 Example of content analysis 117

Preface

Jacky Hong (University of Macau, China) and Jorge Muniz Jr. (Sao Paulo State University, Brazil) first met in the 2012 Organizational Learning, Knowledge and Capability (OLKC) Conference in Valencia. During their first meeting, they started a discussion to identify some possibilities to conduct a joint research project. OLKC is an annual conference that gathers scholars and practitioners in the fields of organizational learning and knowledge management to present and discuss their latest research findings and practice. Since then, the OLKC Conference series has offered an annual opportunity for them to discuss new research opportunities and sustain the partnership.

Sao Paulo State University (UNESP) is listed among the three largest and most important Brazilian universities. UNESP stands out as an example of extreme success among the multi-campus institutions around the world. As one of three public universities maintained by the government of the state of São Paulo, UNESP offers quality education while developing strategic research and interacting with the society through the provision of services for the community.

Founded in 1981, the University of Macau (UM) is an international public comprehensive university in Macao. UM is currently ranked at 322 in the QS world rankings and in the 201–250 range in the Times Higher Education Rankings. UM is an international university with a multicultural campus. It adopts a modern governance model and recruits faculty members internationally. UM has established close strategic partnerships with leading academic institutions in China and abroad, including those in Portuguese- and English-speaking countries. Both UNESP and UM actively engage in internationalization activities to improve the quality of research and teaching.

The 2013 OLKC Conference in Washington had a panel chaired by Professor Mark Easterby-Smith, who gave advices to PhD students and early career researchers about some potential research opportunities related to knowledge management and organizational learning. As a leading figure in organizational learning and research methodology for management studies, he highlighted Brazil, Russia, India, China and South Africa (BRICS) as an important research context for knowledge management during the panel discussions.

Jacky and Jorge subsequently followed his advice to explore this opportunity and launched a research project entitled '*Creating a favorable context for the knowledge sharing of workers: evaluating factors in the automotive plants in Brazil and China*'. This research aimed to evaluate key people, production and organizational factors that influenced knowledge sharing in automotive production context in Brazil and China. The researchers construed that despite a growing recognition about the importance of knowledge sharing in organizations, our understanding about the unique challenges encountered by the blue-collar workers in a production context was rather limited. Also, the research raised some issues and challenges involved for production organizations to engage in cross-national knowledge sharing, which had remained relatively underexplored. There were three Brazilian and two Chinese automotive plants being studied in the empirical work. The significant differences between Chinese and Brazilian workers on the relative importance they attributed to knowledge sharing processes and corresponding enabling factors reinforced our understanding about the challenges of knowledge sharing across cultures and lent a strong support to a more particularistic debate on knowledge management.

In view of the gaps in the extant literature, this research aimed to further identify and evaluate factors that influence cross-national knowledge sharing in automotive production contexts. The research addressed the gaps to promote supportive ways to provide employees' interaction, best practices and lessons learning sharing. The research was funded by the Sao Paulo Research Foundation (FAPESP, # 2016-00132), and National Council for Scientific and Technological Development (CNPq, #309028/2015-9). The research protocol was discussed and finalized at the 2014 OLKC Conference in Oslo, Norway.

In 2015, Jacky came to UNESP, Brazil, as a Visiting Professor. This visit offered a good opportunity for having more in-depth discussions about the research arrangements, visiting Brazilian plants and giving postgraduate lectures. In 2018, Jorge went to UM, Macau for continuing the joint discussions with Jacky, expanding the research scope and sharing the interim results with other academics and researchers.

The fact that both had supervised graduate students whose research was aligned with the broad themes of knowledge management in cross-cultural contexts served as the underlying motivation for the creation of this book. Their research focused on the relationships between cultural factors and workers' knowledge sharing in production plants located in Brazil and China from three different industries.

Currently, industry practitioners and researchers have devoted a growing attention to implementing Industry 4.0 (I4.0) in the production of goods and services. By adopting a multidisciplinary approach, Jorge and Hong's partnership extended to the creation of a multidisciplinary team on Social Systems for Future Manufacturing (SSFM) with researchers from Sao Paulo State University (Unesp, Brazil), University of Macau (UM, Macau) and University of Birmingham (UoB, UK). At the moment, the SSFM research team aims to investigate the impact of I4.0 implementation on the Brazilian, Chinese and English automotive sectors by focusing on factors pertinent to work (e.g., human resources), production (e.g., physical resources used in the production process) and knowledge (e.g., creation and sharing of knowledge among workers). The research project will address difficulties associated with the implementation of I4.0 in emerging economies, including differences in national culture and workers' training.

Investigating how blue-collar workers in their social systems are adjusting to I4.0 is relevant for industrial sectors under transformation in this new technological context. I4.0 demands new professional skills and will affect employment. The automotive sector in Brazil and China is representative of research, thus providing relevant cultural and institutional conditions to support the proposed discussions. It is noteworthy that this research is in line with the Sustainable Development Goals (SDGs) proposed by the United Nations (UN); Quality Education (SDG-4); Decent Work and Economic Growth (SDG-8); and Industry, Innovation, and Infrastructure (SDG-9), which seeks to promote inclusive and sustainable industrialization and foster innovation. The research will contribute to explore in what ways and to what extent the implementation of I4.0 impacts workers' tacit knowledge sharing. Cultural factors impacting on knowledge sharing may stem both from organizational as well as national culture. As organizational culture is influenced by national culture, we need to consider relevant cultural frameworks, which may help us understand international contexts. The research aims to contribute to sustainable organizational practices, formulation of public policies that alleviate social problems and guidance of professional curricula affected by I4.0.

In conclusion, this book celebrates 10 years of productive partnership and friendship between Jorge and Jacky!

Acknowledgements

Jorge Muniz Jr. would like to thank the following research funding agencies in Brazil for their support; grant #2021/10944-2, Sao Paulo Research Foundation (FAPESP); #88887.310463/2018-00 (CAPES-PrInt), Coordination of Superior Level Staff Improvement (CAPES) and #309028/2015-9, National Council for Scientific and Technological Development (CNPq). He would also like to thank Ruben Escobar dos Santos for the creation of graphics.

Jacky Hong would like to express his gratitude for the research assistance on Industry 4.0 in China provided by Xijie Fu.

Acronyms

AHP	analytic hierarchy process
BMN	Brazilian multinationals
BoP	balance of payments
BPPLC	British Petroleum Company Public Limited Company
BRICS	Brazil, Russia, India, China and South Africa
CNI	Brazilian Industrial Confederation
COMEX	Comércio Exterior (Foreign Trade)
EIG	Energy & Infrastructure Group
FDIs	foreign direct investment
GDP	Gross Domestic Product
GE	General Electric
GTMC	GAC Toyota Motor Co Ltd
HRM	human resources management
I4.0	Industry 4.0
ICA	internal communication application
IFDIs	inflow foreign direct investments
ILO	International Labour Organization
IMF	International Monetary Fund
IPC	incomplete pairwise comparisons
KM	knowledge management
MCTI	Brazilian Ministry of Science, Technology and Innovation
MNCs	multinational corporations
NEVs	new energy vehicles
OFDIs	outward foreign direct investments
OICA	International Organization of Motor Vehicle Manufacturers
RMB	renminbi
SECI	socialization, externalization, combination and internalization
UNCTAD	United Nations Conference on Trade and Development

1 Introduction

China and Brazil are two major emerging economies nowadays. Despite facing significant problems in domestic environments, both countries were able to overcome the challenges and embark on the journey of sustainable development through a series of economic and political reforms. As in the case of China, its scale and growth of foreign direct investments (FDIs) were remarkable over the past two decades. With its growing economic influences and the competitiveness of Chinese multinational corporations (MNCs), such as Huawei, Xiaomi and Alibaba, China has joined the ranks of major players in the global market.

In the case of Brazil, its FDI net inflows' trend over the past two decades is similar to that of China (Figure 1.1). Some Brazilian companies, like Vale (mining), Petrobras (gas and oil), Itau Unibanco (banking), Ambev (beverage), Embraer (aerospace), stand out in the international context (Value Today, 2021). As for the automotive industry, Brazil and China are among the top ten car manufacturing countries in the world and have produced around 2.01 and 25.2 million vehicles in 2020, respectively (OICA, 2021).

The first part of the chapter provides an overview of China's economic development with a specific reference to its outward FDIs (OFDIs) and inward (IFDIs) and trading relationships between China and Portuguese-speaking countries, including Brazil. The second part of the chapter reviews the economic developments of Brazil, followed by the discussions of related challenges on cross-cultural knowledge management.

Economic Development of China

Chinese Outward FDIs

Over the past 40 years of market reform and open-door policy, China's OFDIs have grown rapidly. After joining the World Trade Organizations and implementing the 'go global' policy in 2001, China's OFDIs have entered a stage of rapid and continuous development (Table 1.1). From 2002 to 2018, China's OFDI grew at an average annual rate of 28.2%, accounting for more than 10% of the global total for three consecutive years. At the end of 2018, China's stock of

DOI: 10.4324/9781003112136-1

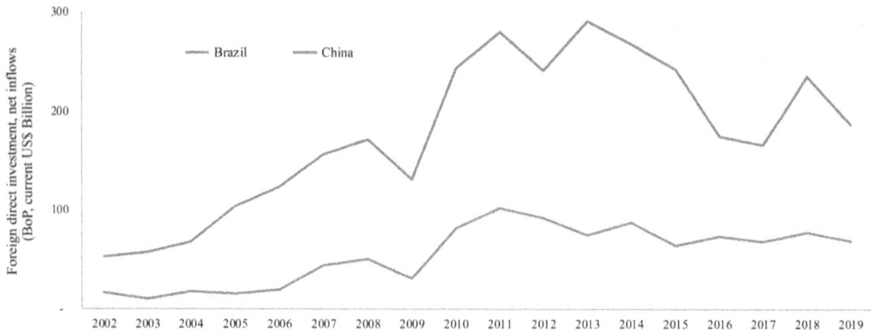

Figure 1.1 Net inflows of foreign direct investment in Brazil and China from 2002 to 2019

Source: International Monetary Fund (2021).

OFDIs had reached US$1,982 billion, representing an increase of $173 billion over the previous year and 66.3 times the stock of OFDIs at the end of 2002. In 2019, China's OFDIs in the whole industry reached US$807.95 billion, showing a slight decrease of 6% year on year. Among them, Chinese domestic investors made non-financial direct investments in 6,535 overseas enterprises in 167 countries and regions with a total investment of US$762.97 billion, down 4.3% year on year.

Table 1.1 Statistics on China's OFDI from 2002 to 2019 (unit: US$100 million)

Year	*Flow*			*Stock*	
	Amount	*Rank (global)*	*Year-on-year %*	*Amount*	*Rank (global)*
2002	27.0	26	\	299.0	25
2003	28.5	21	5.6	332.0	25
2004	55.0	20	93.0	448.0	27
2005	122.6	17	122.9	572.0	24
2006	211.6	13	43.8	906.3	23
2007	265.1	17	25.3	1,179.1	22
2008	559.1	12	110.9	1,839.7	18
2009	565.3	5	1.1	2,457.5	16
2010	688.1	5	21.7	3,172.1	17
2011	746.5	6	8.5	4,247.8	13
2012	878.0	3	17.6	5,319.4	13
2013	1,078.4	3	22.8	6,604.8	11
2014	1,231.2	3	14.2	8,826.4	8
2015	1,456.7	2	18.3	10,978.6	8
2016	1,961.5	2	34.7	13,573.9	6
2017	1,582.9	3	−19.3	18,090.4	2
2018	1,430.4	2	−9.6	19,822.7	3
2019	1,171.2	2	−9.8		

Source: Statistical Bulletin of China's Outward Foreign Direct Investment in 2019.

Table 1.2 Top 20 countries/regions with China's OFDIs in 2018 (unit: US$100 million)

	Country/Region	*Amount*	*%*
1	Hong Kong, China	868.7	60.7
2	United States	74.8	5.2
3	British Virgin Islands	71.5	5
4	Singapore	64.1	4.5
5	Cayman Islands	54.7	3.8
6	Luxembourg	24.9	1.7
7	Australia	19.9	1.4
8	Indonesia	18.6	1.3
9	Malaysia	16.6	1.2
10	Canada	15.6	1.1
11	Germany	14.7	1
12	Laos	12.4	0.9
13	Vietnam	11.5	0.8
14	United Arab Emirates	10.8	0.8
15	Swedish	10.6	0.7
16	Netherlands	10.4	0.7
17	South Korea	10.3	0.7
18	British	10.3	0.7
19	Macau, China	8.1	0.6
20	Cambodia	7.8	0.6
Total		1,336.3	93.4

Source: Statistical Bulletin of China's Outward Foreign Direct Investment in 2018.

By the end of 2018, more than 27,000 Chinese domestic investors had set up 43,000 companies in 188 countries and regions, and more than 80% of the world's countries and regions had received capital and financial investments from China. China has established more than 10,000 overseas enterprises in countries (regions) along the One Belt One Road region. In 2018, the FDI flow was US$17.89 billion and the year-end stock was US$172.77 billion, accounting for 12.5% and 8.7%, respectively. China's OFDI is highly geographically concentrated, with the top 20 countries (regions) accounting for 91.7% of the total amount (Table 1.2).

With the gradual improvement of COVID-19 in domestic environment, Chinese OFDIs are also stabilizing. However, due to the contraction of global value chains and the downturn of global cross-border investments, the pace of the Chinese 'Going Out' policy may need to slow down and the Chinese OFDIs will continue to decline in the coming years.

Chinese Inward FDIs

Apart from promoting OFDIs, China has also made considerable and steady progress in attracting foreign capital investments (Table 1.3). During the period

Table 1.3 China's utilization of foreign capital (IFDI) from 2000 to 2019

Year	*Number of FDI projects*	*Amount of actual utilization (US$100 million)*
2000	22,347	407.2
2001	26,140	468.8
2002	34,171	527.4
2003	41,081	535.1
2004	43,664	606.3
2005	44,001	603.3
2006	41,473	658.2
2007	37,871	747.7
2008	27,514	924.0
2009	23,435	900.3
2010	27,406	1,057.4
2011	27,712	1,160.1
2012	24,925	1,117.2
2013	22,773	1,175.9
2014	23,778	1,195.6
2015	26,575	1,262.7
2016	27,900	1,260.0
2017	35,652	1,310.4
2018	60,533	1,349.7
2019	41,000	1,381.4

Source: Statistical Bulletin of China's Inflows of FDIs in 2019.

from 2001 to 2011, the annual actual utilization rate of foreign investment in China reached US$80.32 billion. Since 2012, China has continued to improve its business environment, with an average annual actual utilization of foreign investment of US$130 billion. By the end of 2018, China had set up about 960,000 foreign-invested enterprises, and the actual utilization of foreign investment exceeded 2.1 trillion yuan, thus reaching 12 times that in 1992 and becoming the second leading country in the world. For the whole year of 2019, there were about 41,000 newly established foreign-invested enterprises in China with the actual utilization of foreign capital of 941.52 billion yuan at an increase of 5.8% on a year-on-year basis.

According to the statistics from the Ministry of Commerce of China, the total amount of foreign investment actually invested by the top ten countries/regions in China reached US$128.46 billion in 2018, accounting for 95.2% of the total amount of foreign investments in the whole country. The top ten countries/regions of China were Hong Kong (US$96.01 billion), Singapore (US$5.34 billion), Taiwan (US$5.03 billion), South Korea (US$4.67 billion), British (US$3.89 billion), Japan (US$3.81 billion), Germany (US$3.68 billion), the United States (US$3.45 billion), the Netherlands (US$1.29 billion) and Macau (US$1.29 billion), respectively.

In the first quarter of 2020, China's absorption of foreign investment has significantly declined due to COVID-19. However, with the epidemic situation soon under control and the whole nation quickly to bounce back to normal, China still remains one of the important investment destinations for foreign investors.

Trading and Investment Relationships between China and Portuguese-Speaking Countries

The community of Portuguese-speaking countries consists of Portugal, Brazil, Angola, Mozambique, Guinea-Bissau, Cape Verde, Sao Tome and Principe, East Timor, Equatorial Guinea, Angola and Mozambique. Based on their special historical origins, the Portuguese-speaking countries have been important economic partners of China. Portugal, as a member of the eurozone countries and European Union, has a long-term economic exchange with China. The total trading volume between China and eight Portuguese-speaking countries (Table 1.4) reached US$149.639 billion in 2019 with 1.55% year-on-year increase. Among them, China exported US$44.064 billion to Portuguese-speaking countries, while China's imports from Portuguese-speaking countries reached US$105.574 billion in 2019.

Among those Portuguese-speaking countries, the bilateral trading volume between China and Brazil was the highest, reaching US$114.680 billion with a year-on-year increase of 3.49%, followed by Angola and Portugal with US$25.365 billion and US$6.643 billion, respectively. However, China's trading volume with other Portuguese-speaking countries, such as Guinea-Bissau and Cape Verde, had a tiny amount of US$280.82 million. Therefore, in terms

Table 1.4 China's foreign direct investment in Portuguese-speaking countries (US$ million)

	Brazil	*Portugal*	*Angola*	*Mozambique*	*East Timor*	*Equatorial Guinea*
2003	6.67	\	0.19	\	\	0.48
2004	6.43	\	0.18	0.66	0.10	1.69
2005	15.09	\	0.47	2.88	\	6.35
2006	10.09	\	22.39	\	\	10.19
2007	51.13	\	41.19	10.03	\	12.82
2008	22.38	\	–9.57	5.85	\	–4.86
2009	116.27	\	8.31	15.85	\	20.88
2010	487.46	\	101.11	0.28	\	22.08
2011	126.40	\	72.72	20.26	\	12.47
2012	194.10	5.15	392.08	230.52	\	138.84
2013	310.93	14.94	224.05	131.89	1.60	22.41
2014	730.00	3.87	–448.57	102.51	9.73	33.13
2015	–63.28	10.72	57.74	68.43	33.81	–13.04
2016	124.77	11.37	164.49	44.25	55.33	–24.91
2017	426.27	1.01	637.55	117.47	19.52	71.11
2018	427.72	11.71	270.34	545.63	10.32	3.80

Sources: CEIC Data, Ministry of Commerce.

of FDIs, China had played a dominant role in Portuguese-speaking countries in recent years.

By joining China, India, Russia and South Africa as Brazil, Russia, India, China and South Africa (BRICS) countries, Brazil is an important emerging economy. It has an enormous geographic market, huge population, rich natural resources and great potential for economic development. Moreover, Brazil is China's largest trading partner in Latin America. According to China Customs, the bilateral trade between China and Brazil reached US$111.181 billion in 2019, representing 27% year-on-year increase. China's exports to Brazil increased to US$33.669 billion in 2019, while the imports from Brazil reached US$77.512 billion, with an increment of 32.3% year on year.

In recent years, Chinese enterprises have increased their investments in Brazil. According to the Chinese Investment Report released by Ministry of Planning, Budget and Management, China has committed 262 investment projects in Brazil in 2018. With a total capital investment of US$126.7 billion, China has become Brazil's largest trading and economic partner.

Economic Development in Brazil

Brazilian Outward FDIs

As a founding member country, Brazil contributes to the International Monetary Fund (IMF) by fulfilling its mission of ensuring the proper functioning of the global financial system through the promotion of international monetary cooperation, exchange stability and economic growth. Currently, in addition to participating as an IMF creditor in lending operations for countries in difficulty, Brazil is subject to regular monitoring of its conditions, preservation and stability of the local financial system as well as taking part in technical assistance and distribution missions and economic advice to other member countries (Brazilian Central Bank, 2021). Its OFDI history (Table 1.5) indicates oscillations related to implementation of economic plans, social programmes, international and/or internal crisis (i.e., presidential impeachments).

Brazilian Central Bank reported that assets of Brazilian companies and individuals abroad (i.e., stocks, bonds, real estate, currencies and deposits or in companies abroad) reached US$558,387 billion in 2020, and there was an increase of 5.5% in comparison with 2019, when assets reached US$529.221 billion. Of the total volume, 80% are direct investments abroad, such as Brazilian companies that have subsidiaries abroad, and this participation reached US$447,991 billion in 2020, an increase of 7.5% compared to the previous year. These investments were made mainly in the Netherlands and in countries known as tax havens, such as the Cayman Islands and Panama. The Netherlands received 21% of the total direct investments made by Brazilians, reaching US$87 billion. In terms of distribution by sectors invested, the highlights are financial services and auxiliary activities companies, reaching US$62.9 billion, as well as oil and natural gas

Table 1.5 Statistics on Brazil's OFDI from 2002 to 2019 (unit: US$100 million)

Year	*Foreign direct investment, net outward (BoP, current US$)*
2002	2.479
2003	0.229
2004	9.822
2005	2.910
2006	28.798
2007	17.061
2008	26.115
2009	–4.552
2010	26.763
2011	16.067
2012	2.083
2013	15.643
2014	20.607
2015	3.134
2016	14.693
2017	21.340
2018	2.025
2019	22.820
2020	–16.419

Source: World Bank (2021b).

extraction with US$12 billion of participation in the capital of direct Brazilian investments (Verdélio, 2021).

Table 1.6 summarizes 190 Brazilian multinationals (BMNs) into 41 economic groups (i.e., automotive, chemical), which control and operate industrial plants abroad. Exports of the 41 BMN groups have a continuous and significant growth throughout the 2001–2013 period, with the exception of 2009 – at an average rate of 12.4% per year. This result was higher than the value of exports of all

Table 1.6 Sectoral distribution of main BMN groups and the exporting companies

Product sector	*Group*	*BMN companies*
Automotive	6	36
Chemicals	5	30
Foods products	5	25
Machines, electrical appliances and materials	3	24
Cellulose, paper and paper products	3	16
Metallurgy	3	14
Others	16	45
Total	41	190

Source: Brazilian Industry Confederation CNI (2020).

companies in the manufacturing industry, which expanded at an annual rate of 10.8%. During the period of decline in Brazilian industry exports, which resulted in a 26% decrease in its value between 2013 and 2019, BMNs' exports also declined, but their fall was less significant (18%). This difference appears in the comparison of the results related to the two trienniums that make up this period. In the 2014–2016 triennium, BMNs' exports declined at an annual rate slightly higher than that of the industry as a whole (−6.9% and −6.5%, respectively). The share of BMNs in total exports by companies in the manufacturing industry has grown continuously since the beginning of the century, increasing from 18.4% in 2001 to 21.9% in 2013 and 24.2% in 2019 (Confederação Nacional da Indústria [CNI], 2020). The Brazilian Industrial Confederation (CNI, 2020) states that participation of BMNs is (1) growing throughout the period, in the machinery, equipment and electrical material sectors; of chemicals; and food products (in this case, with a drop at the end of the period); and (2) presents a certain stability throughout the entire period, although fluctuating within wide intervals, in the case of the pulp and paper sectors, metallurgy and automotive vehicles.

Brazilian Inward FDIs

From a historical point of view (Table 1.7), the attraction of inward FDI (IFDIs) proved to be favourable to the Brazilian economy basically for two reasons: (1) for contributing to the minimization of persistent deficits in current transactions,

Table 1.7 Statistics on Brazil's IFDI from 2002 to 2020 (unit: US$100 million)

Year	*Foreign direct investment, net inward (BoP, current US$)*
2002	16.587
2003	10.123
2004	18.161
2005	15.460
2006	19.418
2007	44.579
2008	50.716
2009	31.481
2010	82.390
2011	102.427
2012	92.568
2013	75.211
2014	87.714
2015	64.738
2016	74.295
2017	68.885
2018	78.163
2019	69.174

Source: World Bank (2021c).

thus closing the balance of payments; and (2) the fact that it boosts internal development with the entry of new technologies, generating employment and income. However, one of the negative points is the repatriation of profits abroad, which causes a persistent deficit in the income account and, consequently, greater pressures on the capital and financial account to balance the external accounts. On the other hand, the global economic expansion drive has made many companies looking for other countries to expand their production, not only concentrating on the export activities but also on the production of goods close to the consumer market or cheaper raw material, be it capital or labour. In this sense, the present theme finds a justification in its study since FDI tends to have a multiplying effect on investments in the economy (Dal Moro, 2020).

FDIs in Brazil increased significantly between 2009 and 2011 and decelerated thereafter. The World Investment Report 2021 (United Nations Conference on Trade and Development [UNCTAD], 2021) indicates that FDI inflows decreased by 62% from US$65 billion in 2019 to US$25 billion in 2020. As a result of the COVID-19 pandemic, Brazil had a significant reduction in FDI in 2020, when the privatization programme and infrastructure concessions were interrupted for several months. The most affected sectors were transportation (which had a reduction in the inflow of more than 85%), financial services (with a 70% drop in inflows), oil and gas extraction (with a 65% drop in FDI) and the automotive industry (which also decreased by 65%). However, there were some significant investments made in the country, even in the midst of the COVID-19 crisis. In January 2021, US-based New Fortress Energy announced that it would acquire Hygo Energy Transition and Golar LNG in a combined US$5 billion deal that marks the group's entry into the Brazilian natural gas sector and makes it the leading gas to power company in Brazil. In addition, as Brazil opens up its natural gas industry to private investors, other major oil companies, including BP PLC and EIG Global Partners, are also seeking multibillion-dollar investments in the country. On the other hand, Ford Motor Co. also announced in January 2021 that it would close the three plants in Brazil and stop producing cars in the country, where it had operated since 1919, as the pandemic increased the industry's persistent idle capacity and reduced the sales, resulting in significant losses. The stocks of FDI have remained stable over the last two years and reached US$608 billion at the end of 2020. Brazil is the 11th largest recipient of FDIs in the world in terms of inflows (6th in the previous year) and the largest in Latin America and the Caribbean. The main investor countries in Brazil are the Netherlands, the United States, Germany, Spain, Bahamas and Luxembourg. Investments are mainly oriented towards oil and gas extraction, automotive industry, financial services, trade, electricity and chemical industry (Santander Brazil, 2021).

Brazil is ranked 124th out of 190 countries in the World Bank's 2020 Doing Business Report, a significant decrease from the previous year, when it was ranked 109th. However, the country is one of the biggest FDI recipients in the world. Brazil is an attractive market for international investors due to several factors: a domestic market of nearly 210 million inhabitants, availability of easily exploitable raw materials, a diversified economy that is less vulnerable to international crises and a strategic geographic position that allows easy access to other South American countries. However, investment in Brazil remains risky because of some negative factors, including cumbersome and complex taxation, bureaucratic delays and heavy and rigid labour legislation. As part of the country's ongoing effort to strengthen its business environment, Brazil introduced electronic certificates of origin which reduced the time required for import documentary compliance to facilitate and simplify the entire process. The country also made several infrastructure concessions which have helped foster investments. The current president has plans for further improving the business environment in the country by implementing administrative reforms, such as decreasing the number of days needed to create a company in Brazil from 79.5 days down to the regional average of 30 days. Easing of regulation in some sectors and potential amendments to the tax system should help as well (Santander Brazil, 2021).

Economic Landscape in China and Brazil

The Brazilian economy has experienced a period of extraordinary growth in its exports driven by an extremely favourable international scenario between 2003 and 2008 (Table 1.8). In addition to the increased demand for various agricultural

Table 1.8 Comparison between FDI inflows and outflows in Brazil and China (unit: US$100 million)

Year	*Exports of goods, services and primary income (BoP, current US$)*	
	Brazil	*China*
2002	73.112	255.970
2003	86.612	462.071
2004	111.797	625.332
2005	137.320	812.612
2006	163.045	1,046.295
2007	195.367	1,341.533
2008	240.186	1,609.656
2009	188.996	1,370.915
2010	249.556	1,798.836
2011	315.251	2,153.120
2012	290.087	2,342.129
2013	292.506	2,539.568
2014	271.696	2,702.274
2015	225.957	2,583.968
2016	230.333	2,424.576
2017	275.689	2,718.976
2018	288.123	2,919.506
2019	285.204	2,904.514
2020	249.587	2,974.046

Source: World Bank (2021d).

and mineral commodities stimulated by the vigorous growth in China, the rise in international prices for these important products in the Brazilian export basket also had positive impacts. While in the period 1990–2002 the average annual growth rate of Brazilian exports was 5.6%, this rate rose to 22% between 2003 and 2008, resulting in high reserves and a reduction in external vulnerability, paving the way for favourable macroeconomic conditions for the resumption of a trajectory of higher growth. The effects of the international crisis, however, caused a significant drop in Brazilian exports in 2009, but the recovery that took place in 2010 and 2011 led the country to a new export record (Hiratuka & Sarti, 2016).

China has been Brazil's most important trading partner since 2009. In relation to international trade, it is characterized by being Brazil's largest buyer and investor. This phenomenon even affects the country's trade balance. Regarding the BRICS countries, which are led by China, Brazil is a very important participant in the block. The ten main Brazilian products exported to China are soy, iron ore, crude oil, beef, cellulose, chicken meat, alloy iron, raw cotton, pork (fresh or chilled) and copper ore and its concentrates. The ten main products imported from China are telecommunications equipment, thermionic valves and tubes, platforms, vessels and other floating structures, organic compounds, transformation industry, machines and electrical appliances, electrical appliances for connection, protection or connection of circuits, parts and accessories for data processing machines, medicines and pharmaceuticals, except veterinary and electric power machines (Varejão, 2021).

Foreign Trade Secretariat of the Ministry of Economy states that in 2020, China became Brazil's most important trading partner by surpassing the historic mark of total trade flows (exports + imports) in excess of US$100 billion. There were exactly US$101,728 billion traded by the two countries. Brazilian exports reached an equal record figure of US$67,685 billion and imports totalled US$34,042 billion (COMEX, 2021).

Forbes Global 2000 list has ranked the world's largest companies in terms of market value on the basis of four equally weighted variables: assets, market value, sales and profits. Table 1.9 shows the top five companies in Brazil and China (Forbes, 2021), which are currently the most representative sectors in both countries.

Brazil and China face different opportunities and challenges (Table 1.10) related to natural resources, labour and internal market conditions.

Employment in Brazil and China

Employment is defined as persons of working age who are engaged in any activity to produce goods or provide services for pay or profit, whether at work during the reference period or not at work due to temporary absence from a job, or to working-time arrangement. The key industry sectors to be considered in our study include mining and quarrying, manufacturing, construction and public utilities, i.e., electricity, gas and water (World Bank, 2021e).

Table 1.9 Top five companies in Brazil and China (US$ billion)

Country	*Name*	*Sector*	*Sales*	*Profit*	*Assets*	*Market value*	*Forbes' rank*
Brazil	Itaú Unibanco Holding	Banking	$37.2	$3.7	$389.7	$48.5	109
	Vale	Materials	$40.4	$5.2	$92.1	$99.2	113
	Banco Bradesco	Banking	$26.7	$3.2	$306.3	$40.9	154
	Petrobras	Oil and gas operations	$52.7	$1.4	$190.1	$53.3	159
	Banco do Brasil	Banking	$24	$2.3	$314	$15.1	272
China	ICBC	Banking	$190.5	$45.8	$4,914.7	$249.5	1
	China Construction Bank	Banking	$173.5	$39.3	$4,301.7	$210.4	4
	Ping An Insurance Group	Insurance	$169.1	$20.8	$1,453.8	$211.2	6
	Agricultural Bank of China	Banking	$153.9	$31.3	$4,159.9	$140.1	9
	Bank of China	Banking	$134	$27.9	$3,731.4	$116.7	14

Source: Forbes (2021).

Table 1.10 Opportunities and challenges in Brazil and China

	Brazil	*China*
Opportunities	• Extensive natural resources • A large middle-class and a large domestic market (fifth largest population in the world) • A strategic geographic location • A diversified economy, well anchored in international exchanges (FDI inflows and foreign exchanges reserves are important, low external debt) • Export sectors, especially in industry, represent investment opportunities, thanks to the weakness of the real exchange rate	• The largest internal market in the world, with 1.44 billion potential customers • Sovereign risk contained as public debt remains mainly domestic and denominated in local currency • Importance of foreign currency reserves and public debt owned by Chinese government and individuals • A well-developed production sector (manufacturing sector and heavy industry) • A favourable geographic location (close to emerging Asian markets, to Japan, maritime frontage) • Top economy in terms of purchasing power parity (PPP), thanks to rapid growth of the economy • Labour costs remain comparatively low, although the situation is changing in certain areas • New opportunities with the development of the western provinces (particularly Sichuan province) • Development of a new export network (Silk Road network)
Challenges	• Onerous labour laws, resulting in high costs to foreign companies and keeping a good part of local business in the informal sector • High costs of production (wages, credit, energy and logistics) • Insufficiently developed infrastructure • High level of regulatory risk (high taxation and heavy fiscal system) • High exposure to changes in commodity prices on international markets • Shortage of qualified labour	• An ever-changing legal environment • Bureaucratic and administrative complexities • A lack of transparency and weak intellectual property rights protection • Ageing population • High level of corporate indebtedness • Production overcapacity in several sectors • A strongly degraded environmental situation in several big cities • Cultural differences in business practices that may be difficult for foreigners to learn and apply in new business situations • Underdeveloped middle management and low rate of qualified workers

Source: Santander Brazil (2021).

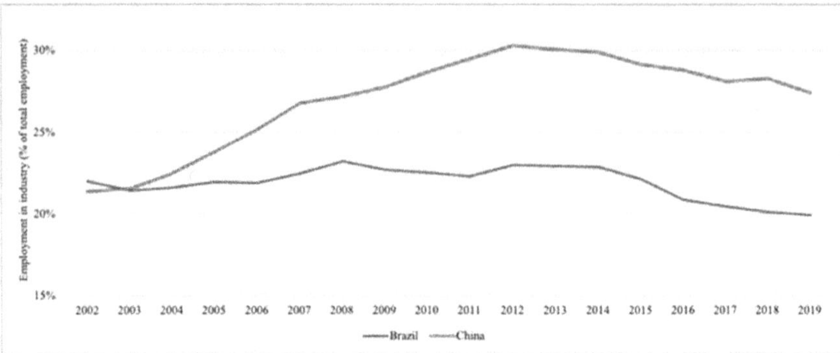

Figure 1.2 Employment in key industries in Brazil and China from 2002 to 2019 (% of total employment)

Source: International Monetary Fund (2021) (Modelled ILO estimate).

Prior to 2002, the contribution of industrial employment in Brazil and China was between 22% and 24%. Figure 1.2 shows the evolution of the proportion of industrial employment in relation to the total number of jobs in Brazil and China (2002–2019). Since 2002, Brazil started to adopt an assessment method from the International Labour Organization, and this year marked the expressive growth in terms of employment in China. It is noteworthy that as of 2012, both countries showed a downward trend in employment in the key industry sectors, and it is common for industrial jobs to decline over time with productivity gains, which has not been observed in Brazil. In 2019 (pre-COVID), Brazil had 19.9% of formal jobs in industry, while there was 27.4% in China.

Industry 4.0 (I4.0) has become an organizational mantra with a promise of significant transformation by integrating processes through new technologies in the plants, and this transformation brings new attributions to workers and the need for their (re)qualification to deal with these technologies. Brazil indicates little focus, priority and allocation of resources for this and acts differently from countries, such as Germany, China and the United States, which have strong leadership for the implementation of I4.0 (Muniz et al., in press).

The development of the worker for I4.0 context involves three issues: (1) competence and skills to handle new technologies, (2) job description related to qualification necessary for the worker to perform new organizational functions and (3) training programmes. These three issues are supported by knowledge management, what is a formal process with deliberate actions to capture, preserve, share and (re)use the tacit and explicit knowledge created and used by people during routine and improvement of production processes in order to generate measurable results for the organization and people (Muniz et al., 2009).

Muniz, Wintersberger, et al. (2021) indicate that workers emphasize the importance of learning from day-to-day practice in solving problems (learning by doing), which makes the process of knowledge conversion between industrial workers a relevant topic.

Challenges on Knowledge Management

In view of the growing economic interdependence and trading relationships between China and Brazil, there is an increasing trend for the MNCs originated from both countries to set up foreign operations in each other's markets, thus intensifying the knowledge sharing and exchange activities. Despite the MNCs from BRICS countries have become more prominent, a conceptual void exists regarding how learning and knowledge management activities take place among members from those national contexts (Hong et al., 2017). Extant research appears to focus mainly on the cross-cultural barriers of knowledge sharing between expatriates and local employees (Hong et al., 2006), and our understanding about the sociocultural challenges on knowledge management among production workers at the shop floor is rather limited (see Muniz, Wintersberger, et al., 2021).

Moreover, prior studies tend to adopt a piecemeal approach by investigating how employee interactions (Zhang & Jiang, 2015), sharing best practices (Mura et al., 2013), interpersonal relationships (Van den Hooff & De Ridder, 2004) and trust (Cleveland & Ellis, 2015; Fteimi & Lehner, 2016) as the enabling factors (Kaasinen et al., 2020; Muniz, Ribeiro, et al., 2021; Rohman et al., 2020) can facilitate knowledge sharing among blue-collar workers. The extent to which managerial perspective is congruent with worker perspectives (Muniz, Wintersberger, et al., 2021; Sanboskani et al., 2020), as well as the organizational issues and managerial challenges involved for production organizations to engage in cross-national knowledge sharing, remains relatively underexplored.

Organizational and sociocultural aspects of knowledge-based studies not only consider processes of generation and exchange of data or information but also consider the social learning processes. This social system influence has a direct impact on the development of a communication system, behaviour and individual learning intent for sharing and acquisition of tacit knowledge (Cleveland & Ellis, 2015; Ingvaldsen, 2015; Reed et al., 2011). Knowledge sharing is relevant for retaining valuable knowledge assets and strengthening the ability of organizations to compete in an increasingly complex, dynamic and knowledge-dependent global business environment (Saini et al., 2017). Developing an effective relationship between managers and employees is difficult, especially when they belong to different cultures. Managers may look biased, illogical and unfair when viewed from the perspective of an employee from another culture (Adler, 2002).

Cross-Cultural Differences

Managing and coordinating the sharing of knowledge and ideas among individual members could be one challenging task in a cross-cultural work environment (Huang et al., 2008). In a cross-cultural setting requiring the sharing of skills and knowledge from a whole range of people, developing a common understanding about what constitutes effective knowledge sharing was crucial for the team in a production context. In particular, members have an obligation to ensure that everyone possessing the requisite information and know-how will contribute wholeheartedly. Prior research indicates the importance for the team members to develop a system of shared interpretations (Nahapiet & Ghoshal, 1998). Under a cross-cultural environment with mutual understandings, members are able and willing to exchange their ideas and knowledge without any fear of negative repercussions. For instance, Tsai and Ghoshal (1998) found that shared understanding can promote resources' exchange and knowledge sharing mediated through trust. Carmeli and Gittell (2009) also reported that a high-quality relationship with shared understanding can facilitate learning from failures by providing psychological safety to foster trust among members for reducing tensions and fears of risk-taking (Inkpen & Tsang, 2005; Tsai & Ghoshal, 1998). Similarly, Sumanarathna et al. (2020) stated that shared understanding plays an essential role in fostering a collaborative environment by mitigating tensions involved during the knowledge sharing process among members from different cultural backgrounds.

Among those production teams where team members come from different cultures, they would have different ways of perceiving tasks and issues at hand (Rivenbark & Frost, 2003). Making the team members overcome the cultural differences while becoming familiar with the vision for the organization as a whole is crucial. By developing a shared understanding about team goals, task and group processes, responsibilities and what each team member brought to the team, a cross-cultural team could also learn how to bridge the chasm. Probably, misunderstandings could also be tempered or softened by familiarity or experience with other cultures (Martin & Hammer, 1989).

Among BRICS emerging countries, Brazil and China are two representatives with high populations, cheap labour and based on industrial consumption (Klafke et al., 2016). Therefore, both countries provide a fertile setting for examining the impact of context-specific cultural and institutional contextual conditions on knowledge sharing in production environments (Muniz et al., 2019; Tong & Mitra, 2009).

Objectives and Structure of the Book

The emergence of China and Brazil as two major developing economies is remarkable. FDIs in these two countries have significantly increased in the last decade, indicating their important economic and political roles in the global market. But scarce attention has been paid to explore how the seemingly different cultural values and norms in China and Brazil appear to affect their knowledge sharing, work and production behaviours.

With these nuances in mind, the present book seeks to address the broader issue of cultural influences on knowledge management. In particular, we aim to (1) identify the factors affecting knowledge sharing activities among the production workers and (2) investigate cross-cultural challenges encountered by both foreign subsidiaries of MNCs in Brazil and China.

The book is structured as follows. Chapter 2 first provides the definitions of knowledge and knowledge management, followed by some issues and challenges in managing knowledge sharing activities across different cultures. Chapter 3 compares different behaviours of knowledge management and sharing between Chinese and Brazilian. Specific emphasis will be put on their indigenous cultural norms, such as *guanxi* and *jeitinho*, and the related impact on the ways they engage in knowledge sharing. Chapter 4 presents the main results of the three qualitative case studies of General Electric (capital goods), Maxion Wheels (automotive parts) and Toyota Motors (automobile) in Brazil and China. Chapter 5 presents the key findings of analytic hierarchy process (AHP) about knowledge sharing activities among Chinese and Brazilian production workers. Chapter 6 then highlights the main contributions of the book and proposes some areas for future study.

References

Adler, N. J. (2002). *International dimensions of organization behavior* (4th ed.). Southwestern.

Brazilian Central Bank. (2021). Available in: https://www.bcb.gov.br/en/about/globalfingovernance.

Carmeli, A., & Gittell, J. H. (2009). High-quality relationships, psychological safety, and learning from failures in work organizations. *Journal of Organizational Behavior, 30*(6), 709–729.

Cleveland, S., & Ellis, T. J. (2015). Rethinking knowledge sharing barriers: A content analysis of 103 studies. *International Journal of Knowledge Management, 11*(1), 28–51.

COMEX. (2021). Comércio Brasil-china rompeu em 2020 pela primeira vez na história a barreira de US$100 bilhões. Available in: https://www.comexdobrasil.com/comercio-brasil-china-rompeu-em-2020-pela-primeira-vez-na-historia-a-barreira-de-us-100-bilhoes/.

Confederação Nacional da Indústria (CNI). (2020). Desempenho exportador das multinacionais brasileiras (Portuguese). Confederação Nacional da Indústria. Brasília: CNI, 2020. 36 p. Available in: https://www.portaldaindustria.com.br/publicacoes/2020/9/desempenho-exportador-das-multinacionais-industriais-brasileiras-2020/.

Dal Moro, O. F. (2020). O Investimento Estrangeiro Direto (IDF) e Seus Determinantes. *A Economia em Revista (AERE), 28*(2), 55–71.

Forbes. (2021). Available in: The World's Biggest Public Companies. https://www.forbes.com/lists/global2000/#39511a435ac0.

Fteimi, N., & Lehner, F. (2016). Main research topics in knowledge management: A content analysis of ECKM publications. *Electronic Journal of Knowledge Management, 14*(1), 5–17.

Hiratuka, C., & Sarti, F. (2016). Relações econômicas entre Brasil e China: análise dos fluxos de comércio e investimento direto estrangeiro. (Portuguese). *Tempo do Mundo, 2*(1), 83–98.

Hong, J., Snell, R., & Easterby-Smith, M. (2006). Cross-cultural influences on organizational learning in MNCs: The case of Japanese companies in China. *Journal of International Management, 12*(4), 408–429.

Hong, J., Snell, R., & Rowley, C. (2017). *Organizational learning in Asia: issues and challenges*. Elsevier.

Huang, Q., Davidson, R., & Gu, J. (2008). Impact of personal and cultural factors on knowledge sharing in China. *Asia Pacific Journal of Management, 25*, 451–471.

Ingvaldsen, J. A. (2015). Organizational learning: Bringing the forces of production back in. *Organization Studies*, *36*(4), 423–444.

International Monetary Fund. (2021). Available in: https://data.worldbank.org/indicator/BX.KLT.DINV.CD.WD?end=2019&locations=BR-CN&start=1999&view=chart. Accessed on: 18 Aug. 2021.

Kaasinen, E., Schmalfuß, F., Özturk, C., Aromaa, S., Boubekeur, M., Heilala, J., Heikkilä, P., Kuula, T., Liinasuo, M., Mach, S., Mehta, R., Petäjä, E., … & Walter, T. (2020). Empowering and engaging industrial workers with Operator 4.0 solutions. *Computers & Industrial Engineering*, *139*, 105678.

Klafke, R. V., Lievore, C., Picinin, C. T., de Francisco, A. C., & Pilatti, L. A. (2016). Primary knowledge management practices applied in Brazil, Russia, India and China (BRIC) industries from 2001-2010. *Journal of Knowledge Management*, *20*(4), 812–828.

Martin, J. N., & Hammer, M. R. (1989). Behavioral categories of intercultural communication competence: Everyday communicators' perceptions. *International Journal of Intercultural Relations*, *13*, 303–332.

Muniz, J., Jr., Hong, J., Oliveira, S., Wintersberger, D., & Popadiuk, S. (2019). Knowledge sharing in the automotive sector: A comparative study of Chinese and Brazilian firms. *Production*, *29*(1), 1–21.

Muniz, J., Jr., Nakano, D., Mello, A. M., Souza, A. A., Lara, C. O., Batista, E. D., Jr., Avelar, E. A., Plonski, G. A., Salve, G. B., Ribeiro, H. J., Jr., Oliveira, J. B., Souto, M. S. M. L., Leite, M. S. A., Salerno, M. S., Trzesniak, P., Marx, R., Boina, T. M., & Lima, W. D. (2009). Gestão do Conhecimento em Sistemas Produtivos (Portuguese). In V. F. Oliveira, V. Cavenagui, & F. S. Másculo (Eds.), *Tópicos Emergentes e Desafios Metodológicos em Engenharia de Produção: Casos, Experiências e Proposições* (pp. 131–203). Associação Nacional de Engenharia de Produção.

Muniz, J., Jr., Ribeiro, V. B., & Pradhan, N. (2021). Knowledge-based assessment applied to lean Brazilian Toyota plants: Employees' perceptions. *International Journal of Knowledge Management*, *17*(2), 1–22.

Muniz, J., Jr., Valentim, M. L. P., Wintersberger, D., Ramirez, P., & Zhang, Y. (in press). The relationship between Industry 4.0 with official Brazilian actions and the 2030 agenda. In: B. M. Fernandes (Org). *Building territories based on GDS leaving no one behind*. EDUNESP

Muniz, J., Jr., Wintersberger, D., & Hong, J. L. (2021). Worker and manager judgments about factors that facilitate knowledge-sharing: Insights from a Brazilian automotive assembly line. *Knowledge and Process Management* (early view). doi: 10.1002/kpm.1693.

Mura, M., Lettieri, E., Rdaelli, G., & Spiller, N. (2013). Promoting professionals' innovative behaviour through knowledge sharing: The moderating role of social capital. *Journal of Knowledge Management*, *17*(4), 527–544.

Nahapiet, J., & Ghoshal, S. (1998). Social capital, intellectual capital, and the organizational advantage. *Academy of Management Review*, *23*(2), 242–266.

OICA. (2021). Production Statistics. Organisation Internationale des Constructeurs d'Automobiles. https://www.oica.net/wp-content/uploads/By-country-region-2020.pdf

Reed, N., Scanlan, J., Wills, G., & Halliday, S. T. (2011). Knowledge use in an advanced manufacturing environment. *Design Studies*, *32*(3), 292–312.

Rivenbark, L., & Frost, M. (2003). Virtual teams that work. *HR Magazine*, *48*(7), 121.

Rohman, A., Eliyana, A., Purwana, D., & Hamidah, H. (2020). Individual and organizational factors' effect on knowledge sharing behavior. *Entrepreneurship and Sustainability Issues*, *8*(1), 38.

Saini, M., Arif, M., & Kulonda, D. J. (2017). Critical factors for transferring and sharing tacit knowledge within lean and agile construction processes. *Construction Innovation*, *18*(1), 64–89.

Sanboskani, H., Kiomjian, D., & Srour, I. (2020). Factors affecting knowledge sharing intentions among construction workers: The case of Lebanon. In *Construction research congress 2020: project management and controls, materials, and contracts* (pp. 171–180). American Society of Civil Engineers.

Santander Brazil (2021). Available in: https://santandertrade.com/en/portal/establish-overseas/brazil/foreign-investment. Accessed on: 18 Aug. 2021.

Santander China (2021). Available in: https://santandertrade.com/en/portal/establish-overseas/china/foreign-investment. Accessed on: 18 Aug. 2021.

Sumanarathna, N., Duodu, B., & Rowlinson, S. (2020). Social capital, exploratory learning and exploitative learning in project-based firms: The mediating effect of collaborative environment. *The Learning Organization*, *27*(4), 351–364.

Tong, J., & Mitra, A. (2009). Chinese cultural influences on knowledge management practice. *Journal of Knowledge Management*, *13*(2), 49–62.

Tsai, W., & Ghoshal, S. (1998). Social capital and value creation: The role of intrafirm networks. *Academy of Management Journal*, *41*(4), 464–476.

United Nations Conference on Trade and Development (UNCTAD). (2021). World Investment Report 2020: Investing in sustainable recovery. Available in: https://unctad.org/system/files/official-document/wir2021_en.pdf. Accessed on: 20 May 2021.

Value Today. (2021). Brazil Top Companies List by Market Cap as on Sep 1st, 2021. https://www.value.today/headquarters/brazil.

Van den Hooff, B., & De Ridder, J. A. (2004). Knowledge sharing in context: The influence of organizational commitment, communication climate and CMC use on knowledge sharing. *Journal of Knowledge Management*, *8*(6), 117–130.

Varejão, P. (2021) Bilateral trade between Brazil and China. Available in: https://www.china-briefing.com/news/bilateral-trade-between-brazil-and-china/. Accessed on: 18 Aug. 2021.

Verdélio, A. (2021). Ativos de brasileiros no exterior ultrapassam US$558 bilhões, diz BC: Ativos são investimentos em ações, títulos, imóveis e moedas. Agencia Brasil.https://agenciabrasil.ebc.com.br/economia/noticia/2021-07/Ativos-de-brasileiros-no-exterior-ultrapassam-us-558-bilhoes-diz-bc.

World Bank. (2021a). What is the difference between foreign direct investment (FDI) net inflows and net outflows? https://datahelpdesk.worldbank.org/knowledgebase/articles/114954-what-is-the-difference-between-foreign-direct-inve.

World Bank. (2021b). Foreign direct investment, net outflows (BoP, current US$) – Brazil and China. https://data.worldbank.org/indicator/BM.KLT.DINV.CD.WD?end=2020&locations=CN-BR&start=2002&view=chart.

World Bank. (2021c). Foreign direct investment, net inflows (BoP, current US$) – Brazil and China. https://data.worldbank.org/indicator/BX.KLT.DINV.CD.WD?end=2019&locations=BR-CN&start=2002.

World Bank. (2021d). Exports of goods, services and primary income (BoP, current US$) - China, Brazil. https://data.worldbank.org/indicator/BX.GSR.TOTL.CD?end=2020&locations=CN-BR&start=2002.

World Bank. (2021e). Employment in industry (% of total employment) (modeled ILO estimate) - Brazil, China. https://data.worldbank.org/indicator/SL.IND.EMPL.ZS?end=2019&locations=BR-CN&start=2002&view=chart.

Zhang, X., & Jiang, J. Y. (2015). With whom shall I share my knowledge? A recipient perspective of knowledge sharing. *Journal of Knowledge Management*, *19*(2), 277–295.

2 Cross-cultural Knowledge Management

Issues and Challenges

Knowledge

Knowledge is defined as a set of structural connectivity and its contents have been proven to be viable for the achievement of organizational goals (Meyer & Sugiyama, 2007). Knowledge means a conscience or norms gained from previous experience upon performing certain tasks assigned or via learning activities, which are gained from observation, reading and dialogue etc. (Parent et al., 2014).

Ullah (2020) revised the definitions of knowledge based on epistemology, engineering design, manufacturing, organization science, information science and education science. According to his conceptualization, there are some concerns about the definitions for being not succinct enough and suffer circularity that claims to be updated. Knowledge thus creates a vast ecosystem by integrating human learning, machine learning, logical inferences (deduction, induction and abduction), experimental data, analytical results, simulations, algorithms, creative thinking and cognitive reflections. The literature on knowledge attributes to the representation of the truth about a subject and/or a set of principles or techniques for negotiating with things or social phenomena. This view is permeated by ideas of social constructivism about the nature of knowledge development (Alvesson & Kärreman, 2001), which considers 'learning while working' and places learning as an integrative part of work in social environments (Easterby-Smith et al., 1999; Nakano, 2006).

Industrial competitiveness and productive systems that have a strong dependence on workers' tacit knowledge need specific strategies for supporting employees from different cultures to work together effectively (Fischer & Smith, 2003). Workers' knowledge was the first barrier faced by 'scientific management' and the withholding thereof is still today a major issue (Webster et al., 2008). Taylorism has increasingly been superseded by new forms of work organizations closely associated with Toyota production principles and supported by creativity and tacit knowledge of workers (Muniz et al., 2021; Thompson & Smith, 2009).

Lean thinking and the Toyota production system place workers' knowledge at the forefront of the processes of continuous improvement and incremental innovations. Processes at the shop floor have required a greater level of participation from the workers involved, who perform a greater range of tasks and

DOI: 10.4324/9781003112136-2

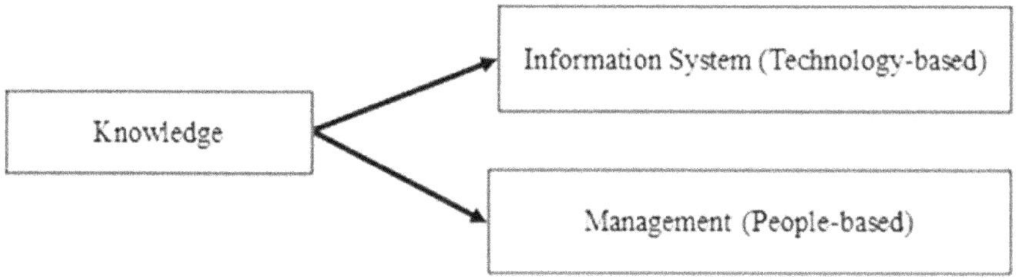

Figure 2.1 Knowledge management and its paradigms

Source: Muniz et al. (2009) adapted from Hazlett et al. (2005); Spender and Scherer (2007).

responsibilities, including the need for specific knowledge and skills as well as the development of autonomy in carrying out production routines and solving problems (Muniz et al., 2022; Wickramasinghe & Wickramasinghe, 2016). Workers' knowledge contributes to the creation and improvement of processes, products and services, which arise as a result of shared experiences, collective sense-making and synergy among workers. Procedures created by the workers themselves to improve productivity and quality increase their engagement on the shop floor (Adler, 1993; Muniz et al., 2021).

There are many sources of knowledge that contribute to improvement in production work performance, including job rotation, employees experience, external partnerships, learning-by-doing, training, suggestion plans, innovations, new practices, product launches, problem-solving methods, continuous improvements (*kaizen*) and hiring. However, it is observed that usually the use of these sources is not an explicit part of the production management models adopted in organizations (Muniz et al., 2010a, 2010b; Wintersberger & Muniz, 2017). Aristotle (Nonaka & Toyama, 2007) indicates three types of knowledge:

- Phronesis: Translated as prudence, practical wisdom, and practical rationality. Faucher et al. (2008) add wisdom to data, information and knowledge based on the traditional classification;
- Techne: Practical and context-specific technical know-how include personal skills with work (craft);
- Episteme: Universal and context-free, objective, and explicit knowledge that can be interpreted as scientific knowledge.

Bisalyaputra (2004, p. 537) states that the critical factors influencing knowledge sharing among workers are poorly understood, probably due to the emphasis on information technology (Von Krogh et al., 2000). Applying Kuhn's (1996) concept of scientific paradigm and following Hazlett et al. (2005) and Spender and Scherer (2007), we classify knowledge management under two approaches (Figure 2.1).

- Technology-based (information systems) related to the importance of data. This computational paradigm emphasizes information technology;

- People-based (management) related to the importance of communication and tacit knowledge. This organic paradigm emphasizes people and their knowledge sharing.

Erden et al. (2008, p. 9) define tacit knowledge at the group level as 'capacity of a group to act as a collective body using their collective mind in situations that are familiar as well as unfamiliar and complex in the absence of explicit rules or directions'. Thus, the tacit knowledge of the group is socially constructed through interactions among individuals or between individuals and their groups in addition to the individual operating in isolation. Socialization occurs, for example, in the relationship in which the apprentice learns the practical knowledge guided by senior operators' dialogue. Erden et al. (2008) define the characteristics of tacit knowledge at the group level as below:

- To be socially constructed;
- To be deeply rooted in action;
- To be dependent on the diversity and cooperation of its members;
- To be embedded in group routines, norms and culture and rooted in commitment, ideals, opinions and emotions. Routines, norms and group culture emerge as a result of shared experiences to guide the collective sense;
- To enable the group to agree on the best action for the 'common good' and find the means to carry it out;
- To enable collective improvisation, which is the group's ability to cooperate and act spontaneously in situations of uncertainty or non-routine.

Erden et al. (2008, pp. 10–11) indicate distinct levels in the quality of the group's tacit knowledge, including:

- Assemblages of people in which members are unknown to each other and without any shared experience. There is a weak group bond with no identity and/or any shared memory, understanding or norms that can be incorporated into the group (i.e., team building of basketball formed with the best players of the states);
- Collective action, which, unlike the previous level, highlights shared events and the development of shared experiences (acting collectively);
- Wisdom (phronesis), the group's ability to find the means to reach a given goal;
- Collective improvisation, the group's ability to cooperate and act spontaneously even in non-routine or uncertain situations. This level of quality is related to the expertise in work group activities, the way in which its members express cooperation and truth, the relationship of the work context with improvisation, culture of experimentation, communication and real-time information and training (Erden et al., 2008; Vera & Crossan, 2005, p. 13).

Knowledge provides support for decision-making and collective actions. Amin and Roberts (2008) present different ways of knowing in action (Table 2.1)

Table 2.1 Varieties of knowing in action

Craft/task knowing	Experience, knowledge, embedded know-how and kinaesthetic awareness are responsible for cultivating shared knowledge. Apprentices learn by replicating a set of tasks within a particular technological, social and cultural setting. Social dynamics sustain knowledge, while colleagues share a specific language, tell stories and build strong bonds of reciprocity, trust and dependence.
Professional knowing	Practice involves implicit relationships, tacit conventions, rules of domain, recognized intuitions and shared understandings. Social interactions include verbal communication, use of artefacts and, to a lesser degree, movement coordination. Knowledge of networks is guaranteed by the presence of professionals, and the exchange of knowledge is informal. This highlights the importance of informal social processes with weak social ties to build, sustain and disseminate knowledge of practices.
Epistemic/creative knowing	A group is formed to experience how new knowledge is constituted, which can go beyond the organization's limits. Examples are groups of researchers, academics, engineers, consultants and product development. This type of group has the challenge of understanding alignment because not everyone is always present in the same social dynamics. Projects are short-lived and professionals' tasks and identities are not shared through working together. Autonomy, improvisation, individual expertise and object orientation prevail. Collaboration tools have to be made with the understanding that social dynamics are based on professional integrity, reputation, weak ties and collaboration architecture arrangement.
Virtual knowing	Online communities are not homogeneous. They exist through poorly structured to complex websites aimed at exchanging knowledge. But there are two types of online interaction and relationship to situational knowledge (CoP): projects that seek innovation that can involve a large number of participants and closed interest groups that face specific problems and are consciously organized as knowledge communities. Advancement in IT is bringing socialization closer and closer so that it can be used by virtual communities of practice.

Source: Amin and Roberts (2008).

underpinning the group's tacit knowledge by referring to the case of communities of practice.

Knowledge Management

Knowledge management is a systematic, formal and deliberate action to capture, preserve, share and (re)use the tacit and explicit knowledge created and used by people during routine and improvement of production processes in order to generate measurable results for the organization and people (Muniz, Trzesniak, et al., 2009). Knowledge management is a complex phenomenon with multiple concepts and processes related to the creation and sharing of knowledge in organizations.

Table 2.2 Different perspectives and characteristics of knowledge

Perspectives	Cognitive	Knowledge is seen as an input that can be stored, combined and reused.
	Constructivist	Knowledge is seen as the creation process itself and is the result of interaction between people.
Characteristics	Prescriptive	Knowledge is intended to advocate actions and principles for changing the organization.
	Analytic	Knowledge is aimed at the elaboration of concepts and constructs that allow the description, analysis and understanding of the phenomenon.

Source: Adapted from Nakano (2006).

Knowledge management contributes to incremental innovation and continuous improvement through an effective utilization of knowledge, which involves elementary changes and more gradual implementation to eliminate wastes, defects, inventories and unnecessary movements, improvement of the layout, work practices and product quality. These innovations are most commonly the result of internal learning processes and accumulated skills. Innovations on the shop floor have become the qualifying factor for competitiveness, and similar attention should be paid to the traditional issues of production and work organization.

Nakano (2006) identifies four different strands in the literature on knowledge and their respective management approaches: cognitive and constructivist perspectives on knowledge, and prescriptive or analytical characters. These differences are described in Table 2.2.

Von Krogh et al. (2000) argue that managers, especially supervisors, should promote knowledge creation in a consistent and systematic way rather than controlling it, and they call this knowledge enabling process, which is the general set of organizational activities that positively affect knowledge creation. The creation of organizational knowledge consists of the process of making available, amplifying, crystallizing and connecting the knowledge generated by individuals to the organization's knowledge system (Nonaka & Von Krogh, 2009, p. 638). Theoretical and empirical works show that knowledge creation cannot be separated from the context in which it is created (Erden et al., 2008; Gilmour, 2003).

Organizational development depends not only exclusively on external influences, but also on internal factors, such as its history, the people who perform the work, existing knowledge, learning processes and the local context itself (Bartezzaghi, 1999). The concern about the conversion of knowledge triggers the ongoing debates regarding the following conceptual issues (Nonaka & Von Krogh, 2009):

- Conceptual foundation in which tacit knowledge is taken as implicit and therefore cannot be transformed into explicit knowledge as indicated in the original ideas of Polanyi (2009);

- Social practice and its relationship with knowledge conversion in which tacit knowledge is acquired through the social practice of solving tasks and resides in these practices. Tsoukas (2003, p. 424) and Hildreth and Kimble (2002) suggest the influence of more experienced people as mentors in carrying out tasks is more prominent. However, it should also be noted that experienced workers have also learned from their interactions with the novices (Fuller et al., 2005);
- Obtaining results from continuous interaction to convert tacit and explicit knowledge has yet to be specified in theory (Gourlay & Nurse, 2005; Nonaka, 1994).

Knowledge sharing is the process where individuals mutually exchange their (implicit and explicit) knowledge, create new knowledge and translate individual knowledge to organizational knowledge (Eze et al., 2013; Van den Hoof & De Ridder, 2004), which is observed in situations involving collaboration between individuals, groups, teams, departments and organizations (Crossan et al., 1999) to achieve common goals and in continuous improvement processes. Knowledge sharing concerns how to transfer expertise and knowledge from knowledge bearers to novices (Hendriks, 2001; Hinds et al., 2001; Kuo & Young, 2008). Tacit knowledge sharing influences organizational performance and competitiveness (Lee & Yang, 2014; Thomas, 2020). Poleacovschi et al. (2019) identify labour characteristics, including hierarchy level, educational background, language and cultural differences as key factors that might explain workers' knowledge sharing behaviours and their intention. Besides, Ding et al. (2017) indicate that relationship, rewards and sense of self-worth influence knowledge sharing intention among people.

Organizations that effectively share knowledge are often more productive than others. Recent studies therefore aim to understand what enables knowledge sharing in organizations (Nakash & Bouhnik, 2021; Thomas, 2020), relating knowledge sharing to HR practices (Sokolov & Zavyalova, 2020), employee engagement (Ahmed et al., 2020), job satisfaction (Rafique & Mahmood, 2018), motivation (Thomas & Gupta, 2021), communication (Parente et al., 2020; Tidström et al., 2018) and organizational performance (Ahmed et al., 2020; Farooq, 2018). However, blue-collar employee perspectives have received limited attention so far (Muniz et al., 2022).

Knowledge management is influenced by many factors, such as culture, leadership and organizational learning (Armaghan & Renaud, 2017; Ding et al., 2017; Hesamamiri et al., 2015). Lee and Choi (2003) indicate the need for organizations to encourage and promote the dissemination and sharing of knowledge between projects in order to encourage specific activities for this purpose. The sharing of knowledge in production management faces different organizational barriers, such as lack of management commitment and trust between people, lack of resources, interpersonal conflicts, underestimation of knowledge contributions from operational levels, ambiguous communication, retention of knowledge as a source of power and intolerance to errors (Devinatz, 2007; Kathiravelu et al., 2013; Riege, 2005; Tonet & Paz, 2006). Frank et al. (2013) indicate that knowledge sharing barriers can be summarized into four types:

- Personal factors are related to individuals and groups concerning their skills, techniques, motivations and strategies;
- Work organization factors which address strategies and practices are related to product development with its methods and activities;
- Technological factors encompassing IT infrastructure, user accessibility and equipment are related to the activities of registering knowledge and information flows;
- External environment involves the subtle influence affecting face-to-face interaction for the exchange of tacit knowledge under great geographic distance between team members.

Thomas and Gupta (2021) and Ahmed et al. (2020) indicate the importance of factors to guide how managers can motivate the workers to share their knowledge with other co-workers. But economic rewards cannot motivate people in the long term. The favourable context of knowledge management needs to connect job satisfaction with knowledge sharing activities (Bavik et al., 2018; Rafique & Mahmood, 2018) supported by managers and workers. Recent literature indicates some research opportunities:

- To understand the factors that support managers to create a knowledge sharing culture (Benyahya & Matošková, 2021; Nakano et al., 2013; Sokolov & Zavyalova, 2020; Thomas & Gupta, 2021);
- To create a knowledge sharing culture supported by a cooperative partnership and engagement between the employer and employees (Ahmed et al., 2020; Benyahya & Matošková, 2021; Ganguly et al., 2019; Nakash & Bouhnik, 2021);
- To guide managers to engage blue-collar workers on the shop floor under a digital transformation context (Ahmed et al., 2020; Manesh et al., 2021; Muniz et al., 2021);
- To determine the extent to which tension–management practices differ in various types of relationships (Tidström et al., 2018);
- To understand how tacit-explicit knowledge conversion influences knowledge sharing (Thomas, 2020).

We adopt the SECI model (Nonaka, 1994) entailing the dimensions of socialization, externalization, combination and internalization, which are considered critical enabling factors to support knowledge sharing. The SECI model has become widely accepted (Alvesson & Kärreman, 2001; Gourlay, 2006; Lee & Choi, 2003) and applied to empirical studies in many contexts, such as the automotive sector (Muniz et al., 2022). And the main application is to support different knowledge management objectives, such as the use of the information for organization learning (Lopez-Nicolas & Soto-Acosta, 2010). Nonaka's SECI model was validated by the practices adopted by Japanese middle managers (Nonaka, 1994).

SECI knowledge conversion process (Nonaka, 1994) driven by social and interpersonal interactions has four ways of conversion: tacit-explicit knowledge conversion may be exemplified on the shop floor as socialization (including dialogue among employees), externalization (codifying the contents of standard operating procedures), internalization (entailing the understanding of standard operating procedures) and combination (summarizing the formal information in standard operating procedures) (Muniz et al., 2019; Muniz et al., 2021; Muniz et al., 2022). However, the support departments (i.e., process engineering) are generally responsible for the combination process and do not involve the operators in the review of standard operating procedures.

Traditionally, production management models are composed of two dimensions, namely the technical dimension and the social dimension. The technical dimension refers to production organization, which is hereafter called the process, including all activities, types and physical arrangement of equipment and the flows of material that result in services and goods. The social dimension refers to work organization, which is hereafter called the people. Knowledge should be considered a third dimension (Muniz et al., 2010a, 2010b; Muniz et al., 2021). Figure 2.2 shows the integrated approach related to people, process and knowledge factors to support better worker knowledge sharing on the shop floor (Muniz et al., 2010a, 2010b, 2019).

Process factors contribute to the control and improvement of the daily activities of workers (Muniz et al., 2022) and include problem-solving methods,

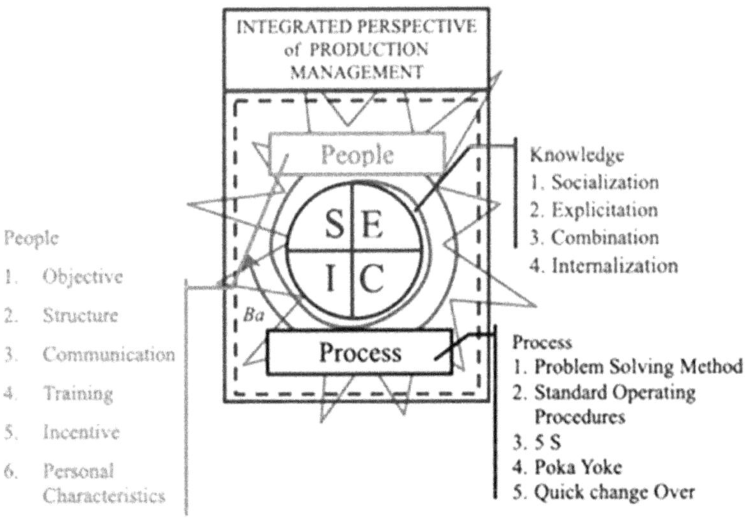

Figure 2.2 Knowledge-based integrated production management model

Source: Muniz et al. (2010a, 2010b)

Table 2.3 Process factors

Process factors	*Descriptions*
Problem-solving method (ASQ, 2021a)	Process of defining a problem; determining the cause of the problem; identifying, prioritizing and selecting alternatives for a solution; and implementing a solution.
Standard operating procedures (ASQ, 2021b)	Set of step-by-step instructions compiled by an organization to help workers carry out complex routine operations. It is a precise description of each work activity, specifying cycle time, the work sequence of specific tasks and the minimum inventory of parts on hand needed to conduct the activity. All jobs are organized around human motion to create an efficient sequence without waste. Work organized in such a way is called standardized work. The three elements that make up standard work are takt time, working sequence and standard in-process stock.
5S (ASQ, 2021c)	Derived from five Japanese terms beginning with the letter 'S' used to create a workplace suited for visual control and lean production. The pillars of 5Ss are simple to learn and important to implement: • *Seiri*: To separate needed tools, parts and instructions from unneeded materials and to remove the unneeded ones. • *Seiton*: To neatly arrange and identify parts and tools for ease of use. • *Seiso*: To conduct a clean-up campaign. • *Seiketsu*: To conduct *seiri*, *seiton* and *seiso* daily to maintain a workplace in perfect condition. • *Shitsuke*: To form the habit of always following the first four S's.
Error proofing (ASQ, 2021d)	The use of any automatic device or method that either makes it impossible for an error to occur or makes the error immediately obvious once it has occurred and has a Japanese equivalent poka-yoke (pronounced PO-ka yo-KAY).
Quick changeover (ASQ, 2021e)	Series of techniques pioneered by Shigeo Shingo for changeovers of production machinery in less than 10 minutes. The long-term objective is always zero setup, in which changeovers are instantaneous and do not interfere in any way with continuous flow. Setup in a single minute is not required, but used as a reference (see 'one-touch exchange of dies', 'internal setup' and 'external setup', also called single-minute exchange of dies (SMED)).

Source: The Authors.

standard operating procedure, 5Ss, *poke-yoke* and quick changeover (Table 2.3), which have been demonstrably found to enable the workers to use and share their knowledge alongside their increasing levels of engagement (Muniz et al., 2021). The use of the process factors enhances the learning of operators by systematically seeking improvements in the production context based on lean manufacturing.

Relevant people factors support the interactions between the operators and the organization by sharing measurable objectives, work, communication, structure and training and incentives (Muniz et al., 2010a, 2010b; Muniz et al., 2021). The people factors include:

- Objectives represent a measurable way to relate the work of the group to the achievement of results by indicating progress, establishing priorities and justifying the claim for material and time resources to be used in problem-solving and improvement projects;
- Structure encompasses the specification of roles and responsibilities of people in the working group, which includes members, group leader and direct supervision and, also, the availability of material and time resources. The formal organization of people, material resources and time allocation stimulate the initiative and the autonomy of the group members to seek support and to meet for creating, sharing, using and assessing new ideas of improvement and results gained;
- Communication is the process by which, ultimately, ideas and feelings are transmitted from people to people, from people to group or from group to group (including to supporting groups, i.e., maintenance and logistics), making the social interaction necessary for knowledge management;
- Training is the skills development in production activities by emulating situations similar to working situations. Training shall provide the working groups with knowledge to action;
- Incentive is related to the stimulus to carry out actions, such as motivating shop floor operators to make suggestions for improvement in the workplace.

Finally, knowledge-related factors include Nonaka's SECI knowledge conversion processes contributing to the creation of a favourable context for promoting knowledge sharing among people, stimulating cooperation and teamwork and emphasizing the importance of converting tacit to explicit knowledge from personal to shared knowledge within the organization. The overall approach stimulates learning through trials and errors.

Knowledge Management in Blue-Collar Workers

Knowledge contributes to enhancing the performance of operations management, allowing the development of high-quality products and services with greater added value and lower cost, increasing the competitiveness of organizations (Yusof et al., 2018). The demands for new products and processes and the decentralization of work promoted by continuous improvement have increased the autonomy and control of tasks for workers (Dawal et al., 2009; Letmathe et al., 2012; Wickramasinghe & Wickramasinghe, 2016).

The tacit knowledge held by supervisors and workers is important to organizations, which is applied to quality control, equipment maintenance and process improvements. Knowledge sharing on the shop floor can be seen at:

- Informal communication related to problem-solving and/or continuous improvement (Nakano et al., 2013);

- New workers' training led by senior ones and/or in communication carried out during daily routines (Knudsen & Madsen, 2014).

Studies show that employees feel greater satisfaction when they have more control over their assignments (Dawal et al., 2009; Letmathe et al., 2012). Job satisfaction generally provides an incentive for operators to work harder and perform better in their activities, helping organizations to be more productive (Wickramasinghe & Wickramasinghe, 2016). Aspects related to job satisfaction are relevant in preventing workers from becoming frustrated (Dawal et al., 2009).

Multi-skilled workers contribute to increasing flexibility and reduced vulnerability of the operation (Philipoom & Steele, 2011; Wickramasinghe & Wickramasinghe, 2016). In general, workers have adapted to different situations and changes (Holm, 2018) and maintained the necessary knowledge to carry out their tasks (Philipoom & Steele, 2011).

Knowledge sharing involves the creation and sharing of knowledge among employees, which implies collaboration and synergy of people to jointly achieve common goals (Van den Hoof & De Ridder, 2004). Knowledge sharing in production systems also faces some significant barriers, such as lack of management commitment and trust among people, lack of resources, interpersonal conflicts, underestimation of the knowledge contributions from bottom levels, threats to self-image, lack of understanding of the organization's processes, ambiguous communication or terminology used, dysfunctional group dynamics (e.g., where people retain knowledge as a source of power), difference in experience levels and intolerance due to past mistakes (Devinatz, 2007; Kathiravelu et al., 2013; Riege, 2005; Tonet & Paz, 2006).

The importance of knowledge, skills and collaborative actions of workers, both novice and experienced operators, becomes relevant in today's increasingly complex production processes (Holm, 2018; Holm et al., 2017; Salomon et al., 2016). Social interaction among blue-collar workers is important to tacit knowledge sharing (Holm, 2018). Personal relationships influence workers regarding the individual decision to share their experiences with their peers, managers and organizations, also taking into account the expectation of obtaining benefits and future incentives in return for such a contribution (Reychav & Weisberg, 2009).

Although having higher autonomy workers may result in greater job satisfaction, it can also generate an increase in tasks and responsibilities (Dawal et al., 2009). There is greater pressure on workers, not only to perform various tasks, but also to continuously engage with new ones (Abdel-Maksoud et al., 2010; Holm, 2018; Tjahjono, 2009).

Under these conditions, Devinatz (2007) indicates that the worker develops strategies of resistance to sharing their knowledge to make the work experience tolerable and, in most cases, these strategies are used to build a space of autonomy in their day-to-day work ('pure and simple' resistance) and not to force management to abandon control practices in the workers' environment (political resistance or 'class consciousness').

Socio-economic aspects, such as the lack of qualified labour and the postponement of retirement due to the ageing of society, affect the implementation of new digital transformation (Peruzzini & Pellicciari, 2017; Shamin et al., 2016) and raise the concerns for managers of productive processes dependent on workers' tacit knowledge (Chen & Fong, 2015; Büyüközkan et al., 2016).

In general, prior studies related to the evolution of industry and operations management do not focus on shop floor operators and their management or organizational aspects (Holm, 2018; Yusof et al., 2018). There is a need for a better understanding of the various factors that affect workers on the shop floor, which has a direct impact on the operational performance and productivity of organizations (Dawal et al., 2009; Salomon et al., 2016; Wickramasinghe & Wickramasinghe, 2016; Yusof et al., 2018). It is worth mentioning that in certain situations, it is disregarded that the success in implementing a technology depends on who applies/uses it, neglecting the role of the worker, who is a relevant player in this process (Di Pasquale et al., 2022; Kipper et al., 2020; Longo et al., 2017).

Prior studies that promote the integration of people, knowledge and production dimensions normally observe tacit and explicit knowledge conversion modes, and they are important in guiding formal procedures to support shop floor knowledge sharing activities. But the conversion process between tacit and explicit knowledge to achieve organizational results is not well specified in the theory (Gourlay, 2006). Tacit knowledge exists, since it is important and needs to be formally observed in a production management system (Muniz et al., 2010a, 2010b; Roy & Mitra, 2018).

Knowledge Management in Cross-cultural Contexts

The previous section highlights the nature and various types of knowledge existing in organizations and corresponding factors affecting its effective management, and the role of knowledge management on the blue-collar worker. People from different cultural backgrounds may, however, have different predispositions about how knowledge management activities can be accomplished and sustained (Bhagat et al., 2002), and their behaviours towards knowledge sharing would vary subject to their national cultural background (Holden, 2001). Accordingly, in this section, after proposing a definition of national culture, we go on to consider the implications and challenges of knowledge management in cross-cultural settings. We conclude this section by identifying some salient cultural values impacting knowledge sharing.

Although the concept of national culture has appeared in the lexicon of various academic disciplines for six decades (Kluckhohn & Strodtbeck, 1961), no single definition can fully encapsulate its diverse meanings and underlying attributes. In our study, culture is conceived as 'a collective programming of the mind' (Hofstede, 1980), which differentiates the members of one group from another. Drawing from an organizational-level perspective, we construe that 'a culture is constituted, at least in part, from the inter-subjective meanings that its members express in their common practice through objects, language, and acts' (Cook & Yanow, 1993, p. 386). National culture may thus shape people's behaviours by providing implicit guidance towards which action should be adopted under specific contexts (Rokeach, 1973; Schwartz, 1992). A person's actions and behavioural tendencies may be driven and influenced by the value systems associated with the indigenous culture in which that person grew up, whereby a value is 'an element of a shared symbolic system which serves as a criterion or standard …' (Parson, 1951: 11–12). As Swidler (1986, p. 283) notes, 'culture provides resources for constructing organized strategies of action', thereby shaping the cognition and behaviours of individuals during their daily encounters.

Driven by the shared value, beliefs and norms, national culture shapes people's behaviours on the basis of national origins (Michailova & Hutchings, 2006). Prior research suggests that national culture-based value differences may give rise to incompatible assumptions about each other's interactive behaviours that can impair knowledge management in cross-cultural settings (Holden, 2001) and may even create some negative impacts (Parkhe, 1991). For example, in a Western-Sino IJVs, the Westerners may see the Chinese partners as change-resistant (Child & Markoczy, 1993) over-preoccupied with 'face' (Ho, 1976), and indifferent to out-groups (Hofstede, 1984), while the Chinese may see their Western counterparts as arrogant and disrespectful (Child et al., 1994). Moreover, socialization appears as a preferred knowledge sharing support mechanism among automotive workers in Brazil, whereas Chinese workers valued more internalization through standard operation procedures. These examples can serve as a strong reminder for 'bringing the culture back' when researching knowledge sharing in organizations (Ipe, 2003).

While such cross-cultural difficulties concern knowledge management at the strategic apex of the organization (Michailova & Hutchings, 2006), our own research, reported later, investigated cross-cultural issues in knowledge sharing at the shop floor level. In relation to specific knowledge sharing activities at the operational level, some host country employees may be reluctant to reveal their locally generated knowledge because of cultural factors and micro-level structural considerations (Hong, 2012). If local employees develop a sense of job insecurity or internal competition, they may come to treat their own knowledge as a 'bargaining chip' vis-à-vis the HQ and other MNC units and withhold it out of self-serving considerations (Mudambi & Navarra, 2004). Other local factors, such as high employee turnover, low levels of employee commitment and lack of incentives, may prevent local knowledge generation and sharing initiatives from getting off the ground (Hong et al., 2014).

According to Hofstede's (1984) framework, differences in national cultural values can be classified into five major dimensions. Among them, two appear as major drivers influencing the motivation and related behaviours of knowledge sharing (Bhagat et al., 2002). First, individualism/collectivism refers to the extent that people identify themselves and are integrated into groups (Hofstede, 1984). The openness in knowledge sharing is reportedly related to the varying levels of collectivism among people. In particular, employees in cultures that are strongly individualistic (e.g., United States) may be reluctant to participate in the collective tacit knowledge sharing with others, whereas employees in strongly collectivist cultures (e.g., China) may prefer not to share knowledge of any kind beyond their immediate circle.

Second, power distance refers to the extent to which people realize and accept the power is distributed unequally in organizations and society (Hofstede, 1984). The existence and perception of high power distance between cultural groups affect the way knowledge is shared among members. Among those countries with high power distance (e.g., China), it is expected for the subordinates to rely on the leaders for constructive knowledge and advice (Hong et al., 2006). In addition, the extent to which a dominant group is willing to consider and entertain the others' perspectives affects the incentive of less powerful group to share their insights (Hong & Snell, 2008).

Therefore, a particularistic approach of knowledge management (Glisby & Holden, 2003) is necessary to explore the differences between Chinese and Brazilian workers about the relative importance of the enabling factors underlying their knowledge sharing processes (Alcântara, 2021; Muniz et al., 2019; Costilhas, 2020). In view of this growing recognition (Tohidinia & Mosakhani, 2010; Wang & Noe, 2010), our understanding about the unique challenges and issues faced by blue-collar workers in production organizations during their cross-cultural knowledge sharing encounters (Muniz et al., 2019; Muniz et al., 2022) is rather limited. This void calls for a better understanding about the challenges of tacit-explicit knowledge conversion in organizations (Erden et al., 2008; Thomas, 2020; Hong et al., 2006; Muniz et al., 2022).

Prior studies have examined key enabling factors for workers' knowledge sharing (Kaasinen et al., 2020; Rohman et al., 2020; Roy & Mitra, 2018; Shirouyehzad et al., 2017). However, while much of the existing research adopts a managerial perspective (Ripamonti & Scaratti, 2012), fairly little is understood about the extent to which managerial perspectives are congruent with worker perspectives (Muniz et al., 2022; Muniz et al., 2021; Nakano et al., 2013). A comparative study between Brazilian and Chinese plants thus offers a good opportunity for encapsulating the enabling factors driving their knowledge sharing activities (Ardichvili et al., 2006; Walczak, 2008; Goswami et al., 2021; Muniz et al., 2019; Ngah & Wong, 2020; Razmerita et al., 2016; Sokolov & Zavyalova, 2020; Souza et al., 2020; Thomas & Gupta, 2021). Through this research opportunity, we aim to address this shortcoming from a shop floor context with insights obtained from blue-collar workers who perform highly interdependent tasks and have heavy reliance on their tacit knowledge.

References

Abdel-Maksoud, A., Cerbioni, F., Ricceri, F., & Velayutham, S. (2010). Employee morale, non-financial performance measures, deployment of innovative managerial practices and shop-floor involvement in Italian manufacturing firms. *The British Accounting Review*, *42*(1), 36–55.

Adler, P. S. (1993). Time-and-motion regained. *Harvard Business Review*, *71*(1), 97–108.

Ahmed, T., Shahid Khan, M., Thitivesa, D., Siraphatthada, Y., & Phumdara, T. (2020). Impact of employees engagement and knowledge sharing on organizational performance: Study of HR challenges in COVID-19 pandemic. *Human Systems Management*, *39*(4), 589–601.

Alcântara, M. B. S. A. (2021). Cultura e Gestão do Conhecimento: um estudo comparativo em fábricas de rodas no Brasil e na China [Portuguese]; Culture and Knowledge Management: a comparative study of wheel factories in Brazil and China [Master's thesis]. School of Engineering of Guaratingueta, Sao Paulo State University, UNESP Repository.

Alvesson, M., & Kärreman, D. (2001). Odd couple: Making sense of the curious concept of knowledge management. *Journal of Management Studies*, *38*(7), 995–1018.

Amin, A., & Roberts, J. (2008). Knowing in action: Beyond communities of practice. *Research Policy*, *37*(2), 353–369.

Ardichvili, A., Maurer, M., Li, W., Wentling, T., & Stuedemann, R. (2006). Cultural influences on knowledge sharing through online communities of practice. *Journal of Knowledge Management*, *10*(1), 94–107.

Armaghan, N., & Renaud, J. (2017). Evaluation of knowledge management in an organization. *Journal of Information & Knowledge Management*, *16*(1), 1750006.

ASQ (2021a). *What is problem solving?* Available: https://asq.org/quality-resources/problem-solving.

ASQ (2021b). *Glossary standard work*. Available in: https://asq.org/quality-resources/quality-glossary/s.

ASQ (2021c). *Glossary five S's (5S)*. Available in: https://asq.org/quality-resources/quality-glossary/f.

ASQ (2021d). *Glossary mistake proofing*. https://asq.org/quality-resources/quality-glossary/m.

ASQ (2021e). *Glossary single-minute exchange of dies*. https://asq.org/quality-resources/quality-glossary/s.

Bartezzaghi, E. (1999). The evolution of production models: Is a new paradigm emerging? *International Journal of Operations & Production Management*, *19*(2), 229–250.

Bavik, Y. L., Tang, P. M., Shao, R., & Lam, L. W. (2018). Ethical leadership and employee knowledge sharing: Exploring dual-mediation paths. *The Leadership Quarterly*, *29*(2), 322–332.

Benyahya, P., & Matošková, J. (2021). Partnership between the employer and the staff as a vital factor for knowledge sharing. *International Journal of Learning and Intellectual Capital*, *18*(1), 5–27.

Bhagat, R., Kedia, B., Harveston, P., & Triandis, H. (2002). Cultural variations in the cross-border transfer of organizational knowledge: An integrative approach. *Academy of Management Review*, *27*, 204–221.

Bisalyaputra, K. (2004, October). Knowledge transfer as sustainable competitive advantage. In *2004 IEEE International Engineering Management Conference* (IEEE Cat. No. 04CH37574) (v2, 536–540). IEEE.

Büyüközkan, G., Parlak, I. B., & Tolga, A. C. (2016). Evaluation of knowledge management tools by using an interval type-2 fuzzy TOPSIS method. *International Journal of Computational Intelligence Systems*, *9*(5), 812–826.

Chen, L., & Fong, P. S. (2015). Evaluation of knowledge management performance: An organic approach. *Information & Management*, *52*(4), 431–453.

Child, J., & Markoczy, L. (1993). Host-country managerial behaviour and learning in Chinese and Hungarian joint ventures. *Journal of Management Studies*, *30*(4), 611–631.

Child, J., Markoczy, L., & Cheung, T. (1994). Managerial adaptation in Chinese and Hungarian strategic alliances with culturally distinct foreign partners. *Advances in Chinese Industrial Studies*, *4*, 211–231.

Cook, S. D. N., & Yanow, D. (1993). Culture and organizational learning. *Journal of Management Inquiry*, *2*, 373–390.

Costilhas, A. A. M. (2020). Workers knowledge sharing improvements and the cultural influence: comparative study Brazil and China in a capital good industry [Master's thesis]. School of Engineering of Guaratingueta, Sao Paulo State University, Unesp Repository: https://repositorio.unesp.br/handle/11449/202394.

Crossan, M. M., Lane, H. W., & White, R. E. (1999). An organizational learning framework: From intuition to institution. *Academy of Management Review*, *24*(3), 522–537.

Dawal, S. Z., Taha, Z., & Ismail, Z. (2009). Effect of job organization on job satisfaction among shop floor employees in automotive industries in Malaysia. *International Journal of Industrial Ergonomics*, *39*(1), 1–6.

Devinatz, V. (2007). Manufacturing resistance: Rationalizing the irrationality of managerial control on the shop floor in a US medical electronics factory. *Employee Responsibilities and Rights Journal*, *19*(1), 1–15.

Di Pasquale, V., De Simone, V., Miranda, S., & Riemma, S. (2022). Smart operators: How augmented and virtual technologies are affecting the worker's performance in manufacturing contexts. *Journal of Industrial Engineering and Management*, *15*(2), 233–255.

Ding, G., Liu, H., Huang, Q., & Gu, J. (2017). Moderating effects of guanxi and face on the relationship between psychological motivation and knowledge-sharing in China. *Journal of Knowledge Management*, *21*(5), 1077–1097.

Easterby-Smith, M., Araujo, L., & Burgoyne, J. (Eds.). (1999). *Organizational learning and the learning organization: Developments in theory and practice*. Sage.

Erden, Z., Von Krogh, G., & Nonaka, I. (2008). The quality of group tacit knowledge. *Journal of Strategic Information Systems*, *17*(1), 4–18.

Eze, U. C., Goh, G. G. G., Goh, C. Y., & Tan, T. L. (2013). Perspectives of SMEs on knowledge sharing. *Journal of Information and Knowledge Management Systems*, *43*(2), 210–236.

Farooq, R. (2018). Developing a conceptual framework of knowledge management. *International Journal of Innovation Science*, *11*(1), 139–160.

Faucher, J. P. L., Everett, A. M., & Lawson, R. (2008). Reconstituting knowledge management. *Journal of Knowledge Management*, *12*(3), 3–12.

Fischer, R., & Smith, P. B. (2003). Reward allocation and culture: A meta-analysis. *Journal of Cross-Cultural Psychology*, *34*(3), 251–268.

Frank, A. G., Ribeiro, J. L. D., Echeveste, M. E., & Caten, C. S. T. (2013). Relação entre características empresariais e fatores da transferência de conhecimentos entre projetos de produto (Portuguese). *Production*, *23*, 95–106.

Fuller, A., Hodkinson, H., Hodkinson, P., & Unwin, L. (2005). Learning as peripheral participation in communities of practice: A reassessment of key concepts in workplace learning. *British Educational Research Journal*, *31*(1), 49–68.

Ganguly, A., Talukdar, A., & Chatterjee, D. (2019). Evaluating the role of social capital, tacit knowledge sharing, knowledge quality and reciprocity in determining innovation capability of an organization. *Journal of Knowledge Management*, *23*(6), 1105–1135.

Gilmour, D. (2003). How to fix knowledge management. *Harvard Business Review*, *81*(10), 16–16.

Glisby, M., & Holden, N. (2003). Contextual constraints in knowledge management theory: The cultural embeddedness of Nonaka's knowledge-creating company. *Knowledge and Process Management*, *10*(1), 29–36.

Goswami, A. K., Agrawal, R. K., & Goswami, M. (2021). Influence of national culture on knowledge management process: Literature review and research agenda. *Benchmarking: An International Journal, 28*(4), 1186–1212.

Gourlay, S. (2006). Conceptualizing knowledge creation: A critique of Nonaka's theory. *Journal of Management Studies, 43*(7), 1415–1436.

Gourlay, S., & Nurse, A. (2005). Flaws in the "engine" of knowledge creation: A critique of Nonaka's theory. *Challenges and issues in knowledge management*, IAP Press, 293–316.

Hazlett, S. A., Mcadam, R., & Gallagher, S. (2005). Theory building in knowledge management: In search of paradigms. *Journal of Management Inquiry, 14*(1), 31–42.

Hendriks, P. (2001). Many rivers to cross: From ICT to knowledge management systems. *Journal of Information Technology, 16*(2), 57–72.

Hesamamiri, R., Mazdeh, M. M., Jafari, M., & Shahanaghi, K. (2015). Knowledge management reliability assessment: An empirical investigation. *Aslib Journal of Information Management, 67*(4), 422.

Hildreth, P. M., & Kimble, C. (2002). The duality of knowledge. *Information Research, 8*(1), 22–34.

Hinds, P. J., Patterson, M., & Pfeffer, J. (2001). The effect of expertise on knowledge transfer and subsequent novice performance. *Applied Psychology, 86*(6), 1232–1243.

Ho, D. Y. (1976). On the concept of face. *American Journal of Sociology, 81*(4), 867–884.

Hofstede, G. (1980). Culture and organizations. *International Studies of Management & Organization, 10*(4), 15–41.

Hofstede, G. (1984). *Culture's consequences: International differences in work-related values.* Beverly Hills.

Holden, N. (2001). Knowledge management: Raising the spectre of the cross-cultural dimension. *Knowledge and Process Management, 8*(3), 155–163.

Holm, M. (2018). The future shop-floor operators, demands, requirements and interpretations. *Journal of Manufacturing Systems, 47*, 35–42.

Holm, M., Danielsson, O., Syberfeldt, A., Moore, P., & Wang, L. (2017). Adaptive instructions to novice shop-floor operators using augmented reality. *Journal of Industrial and Production Engineering, 34*(5), 362–374.

Hong, J. (2012). Nonaka's SECI model: Issues and challenges. *Management Learning, 43*(2), 199–215.

Hong, J., & Snell, R. (2008). Power inequality in cross-cultural learning: The case of Japanese transplants in China. *Asia Pacific Business Review, 14*(2), 253–273.

Hong, J., Snell, R., & Easterby-Smith, M. (2006). Cross cultural influences of organizational learning in MNCs: The case of Japanese companies in China. *Journal of International Management, 12*(4), 408–429.

Hong, J., Snell, R., & Mak, C. (2014). Contextualizing Nonaka's theory of knowledge in China: When Samurai meets Bruce Lee. In A. Örtenblad (Ed.), *Handbook of research on knowledge management: Adaptation and context* (pp. 343–365). Edward Elgar.

Ipe, M. (2003). Knowledge sharing in organizations: A conceptual framework. *Human Resource Development Review, 2*(4), 337–359.

Kaasinen, E., Schmalfuß, F., Özturk, C., Aromaa, S., Boubekeur, M., Heilala, J., & Walter, T. (2020). Empowering and engaging industrial workers with Operator 4.0 solutions. *Computers & Industrial Engineering, 139*, 105678.

Kathiravelu, S. R., Mansor, N., & Kenny, K. (2013). Factors influencing knowledge sharing behaviour among employees of public services in Malaysia. *International Journal of Academic Research in Economics and Management Sciences, 2*(3), 107–119.

Kipper, L. M., Furstenau, L. B., Hoppe, D., Frozza, R., & Iepsen, S. (2020). Scopus scientific mapping production in Industry 4.0 (2011–2018): A bibliometric analysis. *International Journal of Production Research, 58*(6), 1605–1627.

Kluckhohn, F., & Strodtbeck, F. (1961). *Variations in value dimensions.* Row & Peterson.

Knudsen, M. P., & Madsen, E. S. (2014). The managerial issues related to transferring shop floor knowledge in manufacturing relocation. *International Journal of Operations & Production Management, 34*(11), 1389–1416.

Kuhn, T. S. *The structure of scientific revolutions* (3rd ed.). The University of Chicago Press, 1996.

Kuo, F., & Young, M. (2008). Predicting knowledge sharing practices through intention: A test of competing models. *Computers in Human Behavior, 24*(6), 2697–2722.

Lee, H., & Choi, B. (2003). Knowledge management enablers, processes, and organizational performance: An integrative view and empirical examination. *Journal of Management Information Systems, 20*(1), 179–228.

Lee, Y. M., & Yang, C. (2014). The relationships among network ties, organizational agility, and organizational performance: A study of the flat glass industry in Taiwan. *Journal of Management and Organization, 20*(2), 206–226.

Letmathe, P., Schweitzer, M., & Zielinski, M. (2012). How to learn new tasks: Shop floor performance effects of knowledge transfer and performance feedback. *Journal of Operations Management, 30*(3), 221–236.

Longo, F., Nicoletti, L., & Padovano, A. (2017). Smart operators in Industry 4.0: A human-centered approach to enhance operators' capabilities and competencies within the new smart factory context. *Computers & Industrial Engineering, 113*, 144–159.

Lopez-Nicolas, C., & Soto-Acosta, P. (2010). Analyzing ICT adoption and use effects on knowledge creation: An empirical investigation in SMEs. *International Journal of Information Management, 30*(6), 521–528.

Manesh, M. F., Pellegrini, M. M., Marzi, G., & Dabic, M. (2021). Knowledge management in the fourth industrial revolution: Mapping the literature and scoping future avenues. *IEEE Transactions on Engineering Management, 68*(1), 289–300.

Meyer, B., & Sugiyama, K. (2007). The concept of knowledge in KM: A dimensional model. *Journal of Knowledge Management, 11*(1), 17–35.

Michailova, S., & Hutchings, K. (2006). National cultural influences on knowledge sharing: A comparison of China and Russia. *Journal of Management Studies, 43*(3), 383–405.

Mudambi, R., & Navarra, P. (2004). Is knowledge power? Knowledge flows, subsidiary power, and rent-seeking within MNCs. *Journal of International Business Studies, 35*(5), 385–406.

Muniz, J., Jr., Batista, E. D., Jr., & Loureiro, G. (2010a). Knowledge-based integrated production management model applied to automotive companies. *International Journal of Knowledge Management Studies, 4*(3), 301–318.

Muniz, J., Jr., Batista, E. D., Jr., & Loureiro, G. (2010b). Knowledge-based integrated production management model. *Journal of Knowledge Management, 14*(6), 858–871.

Muniz, J., Jr., Hong, J., Oliveira, S., Wintersberger, D., & Popadiuk, S. (2019). Knowledge sharing in the automotive sector: A comparative study of Chinese and Brazilian firms. *Production, 29*(1), 1–21.

Muniz, J., Jr., Nakano, D., Mello, A. M., Souza, A. A., Lara, C. O., Batista, E. D., Jr., Avelar, E. A., Plonski, G. A., Salve, G. B., Ribeiro, H. J., Jr., Oliveira, J. B., Souto, M. S. M. L., Leite, M. S. A., Salerno, M. S., Trzesniak, P., Marx, R., Boina, T. M., & Lima, W. D. (2009). Knowledge management in the production systems. (Gestão do conhecimento em sistemas produtivos, Portuguese). In V. F. Oliveira, V. Cavenagui, & F. S.

Másculo(org) (Eds.), *Emerging topics and methodologies challenges in production engineering: cases, experiences and propositions II (Tópicos Emergentes e Desafios Metodológicos em Engenharia de Produção: Casos, Experiências e Proposições, Portuguese)*. ABEPRO, 2, pp. 131–203.

Muniz, J., Jr., Ribeiro, V. B., & Pradhan, N. (2021). Knowledge-based assessment applied to lean Brazilian Toyota plants: Employees' perceptions. *International Journal of Knowledge Management, 17*(2), 1–22.

Muniz, J., Jr., Trzesniak, P., & Batista Jr., E. D. (2009). An definitive concept to knowledge management: need to science evolution and effectiveness application (Um enunciado definitivo para o conceito de gestão do conhecimento: necessidade para o avanço da ciência e para a aplicação eficaz, Portuguese). In V. F. Oliveira, V. Cavenagui, & F. S. Másculo(org) (Eds.), *Emerging topics and methodologies challenges in production engineering: cases, experiences and propositions II (Tópicos Emergentes e Desafios Metodológicos em Engenharia de Produção: Casos, Experiências e Proposições, Portuguese)*. ABEPRO, 2, pp. 137–145.

Muniz Jr, J., Wintersberger, D., & Hong, J. L. (2022). Worker and manager judgments about factors that facilitate knowledge-sharing: Insights from a Brazilian automotive assembly line. *Knowledge and Process Management, 29*(2), 132–146.

Nakano, D. (2006). Reframing Knowledge Management: a study of perspectives and related processes. In: *2nd. European Conference on Management of Technology Proceedings*, Birmingham: Proceedings.

Nakano, D., Muniz, J., Jr., & Batista, E. D., Jr. (2013). Engaging environments: Tacit knowledge sharing on the shop floor. *Journal of Knowledge Management, 17*(2), 290–306.

Nakash, M., & Bouhnik, D. (2021). Knowledge management is not dead. It has changed its appearance. And it will continue to change. *Knowledge and Process Management, 28*(1), 29–39.

Ngah, R., & Wong, K. Y. (2020). Linking knowledge management to competitive strategies of knowledge-based SMEs. *The Bottom Line, 33*(1), 42–59.

Nonaka, I. (1994). A dynamic theory of organizational knowledge creation. *Organization Science, 5*(1), 14–37.

Nonaka, I., & Von Krogh, G. (2009). Perspective—Tacit knowledge and knowledge conversion: Controversy and advancement in organizational knowledge creation theory. *Organization Science, 20*(3), 635–652.

Nonaka, I., & Toyama, R. (2007). Strategic management as distributed practical wisdom (phronesis). *Industrial and Corporate Change, 16*(3), 371–394.

Parent, M. M., MacDonald, D., & Goulet, G. (2014). The theory and practice of knowledge management and transfer: The case of the Olympic Games. *Sport Management Review, 17*(2), 205–218.

Parente, R., Murray, J. Y., Zhao, Y., Kotabe, M., & Dias, R. (2020). Relational resources, tacit knowledge integration capability, and business performance. *Journal of Knowledge Management*. doi: 10.1108/JKM-07-2020-0501.

Parkhe, A. (1991). Interfirm diversity, organizational, learning and longevity in global strategic alliance. *Journal of International Business Studies, 4*, 579–601.

Parson, T. (1951). *The social system*. Free Press.

Peruzzini, M., & Pellicciari, M. (2017). A framework to design a human-centred adaptive manufacturing system for aging workers. *Advanced Engineering Informatics, 33*, 330–349.

Philipoom, P., & Steele, D. (2011). Shop floor control when tacit worker knowledge is important. *Decision Sciences, 42*(3), 655–688.

Polanyi, M. (2009). *The tacit dimension*. Chicago: University of Chicago Press.

Poleacovschi, C., Javernick-Will, A., Tong, T., & Wanberg, J. (2019). Engineers seeking knowledge: Effect of control systems on accessibility of tacit and codified knowledge. *Journal of Construction Engineering and Management*, *145*(2), 04018128.

Rafique, G. M., & Mahmood, K. (2018). Relationship between knowledge sharing and job satisfaction: A systematic review. *Information and Learning Sciences*, *119*(5/6), 295–312.

Razmerita, L., Kirchner, K., & Nielsen, P. (2016). What factors influence knowledge sharing in organizations? A social dilemma perspective of social media communication. *Journal of Knowledge Management*, *20*(6), 1225–1246.

Reychav, I., & Weisberg, J. (2009). Good for workers, good for companies: How knowledge sharing benefits individual employees. *Knowledge and Process Management*, *16*(4), 186–197.

Riege, A. (2005). Three-dozen knowledge-sharing barriers managers must consider. *Journal of Knowledge Management*, *9*(3), 18–35.

Ripamonti, S., & Scaratti, G. (2012). Weak knowledge for strengthening competences: A practice-based approach in assessment management. *Management Learning*, *43*(2), 183–197.

Rohman, A., Eliyana, A., Purwana, D., & Hamidah, H. (2020). Individual and organizational factors' effect on knowledge sharing behavior. *Entrepreneurship and Sustainability Issues*, *8*(1), 38–48.

Rokeach, M. (1973). *The nature of human values*. Free Press.

Roy, S., & Mitra, J. (2018). Tacit and explicit knowledge management and assessment of quality performance of public R&D in emerging economies: An Indian perspective. *Journal of Organizational Change Management*, *31*(1), 188–214.

Salomon, V. A., Simon, M. L., & Muniz, J., Jr. (2016). Complexity and operations performance: A case study. *Annals of Management Science*, *5*(1), 93.

Schwartz, S. H. (1992). Universals in the content and structure of values: Theoretical advances and empirical tests in 20 countries. In: M. Zanna (Ed.), *Advances in experimental social psychology*, 25, Academic Press, New York.

Shamim, S., Cang, S., Yu, H., & Li, Y. (2016, July). Management approaches for Industry 4.0: A human resource management perspective. In 2016 *IEEE Congress on Evolutionary Computation* (CEC) (pp. 5309–5316). IEEE.

Shirouyehzad, H., Rafiee, F. M., & Berjis, N. (2017). Performance evaluation and prioritization of organizations based on knowledge management and safety management approaches using DEA, a case study. *Journal of Modelling in Management*, *12*(1), 77–95.

Sokolov, D., & Zavyalova, E. (2020). Human resource management systems and intellectual capital: Is the relationship universal in knowledge-intensive firms? *International Journal of Manpower*, *42*(4), 683–701.

Souza, D. S. D. O. A., Salgado, A. M. P., Marins, F. A. S., & Muniz, J., Jr. (2020). The influence of leaders' characteristics on the relationship between leadership and knowledge management. *Knowledge Management Research & Practice*, *18*(4), 462–473.

Spender, J. C., & Scherer, A. G. (2007). The philosophical foundations of knowledge management: Editor's introduction. *Organization*, *14*(1), 1–30.

Swidler, A. (1986). Culture in action: Symbols and strategies. *American Sociological Review*, *51*, 273–286.

Thomas, A., & Gupta, V. (2021). The role of motivation theories in knowledge sharing: An integrative theoretical reviews and future research agenda. *Kybernetes*, *51*(1), 116–140.

Thomas, N. (2020). Debates around the nature of knowledge transfer: How well do we know about the construct? *VINE Journal of Information and Knowledge Management Systems*, *50*(3), 409–425.

Thompson, P., & Smith, C. (2009). Labour power and labour process: Contesting the marginality of the sociology of work. *Sociology*, *43*(5), 913–930.

Tidström, A., Ritala, P., & Lainema, K. (2018). Interactional and procedural practices in managing coopetitive tensions. *Journal of Business & Industrial Marketing*, *33*(7), 945–957.

Tjahjono, B. (2009). Supporting shop floor workers with a multimedia task-oriented information system. *Computers in Industry*, *60*(4), 257–265.

Tohidinia, Z., & Mosakhani, M. (2010). Knowledge sharing behaviour and its predictors. *Industrial Management & Data Systems*, *110*(4), 611–631.

Tonet, H. C., & Paz, M. G. T. (2006). Um modelo para o compartilhamento de conhecimento no trabalho. *Revista de Administração Contemporânea*, *10*(2), 75–94.

Tsoukas, H. (2003). Do we really understand tacit knowledge? In M. Easterby-Smith, & M. Lyles (Eds.), *Handbook of OrganizationalLearning and knowledge management* (pp. 410–427). Blackwell.

Ullah, A. S. (2020). What is knowledge in Industry 4.0? *Engineering Reports*, *2*(8), e12217.

Van den Hoof, B., & De Ridder, J. A. (2004). Knowledge sharing in context: The influence of organizational commitment, communication climate and CMC use on knowledge sharing. *Journal of Knowledge Management*, *8*(6), 117–130.

Vera, D., & Crossan, M. (2005). Improvisation and innovative performance in teams. *Organization Science*, *16*(3), 203–224.

Von Krogh, G., Ichijo, K., & Nonaka, I. (2000). *Enabling knowledge creation: How to unlock the mystery of tacit knowledge and release the power of innovation*. Oxford University Press on Demand.

Walczak, S. (2008). Knowledge management and organizational learning. *Learning Organization*, *15*(6), 486–494.

Wang, S., & Noe, R. A. (2010). Knowledge sharing: A review and directions for future research. *Human Resource Management Review*, *20*(2), 115–131.

Webster, J., Brown, G., Zweig, D., Connelly, C. E., Brodt, S., & Sitkin, S. (2008). Beyond knowledge sharing: Withholding knowledge at work. In J. J. Martocchio (Ed.), *Research in personnel and human resources management* (Vol. 27, pp. 1–37). Emerald Group Publishing Limited.

Wickramasinghe, V., & Wickramasinghe, G. L. D. (2016). Variable pay and job performance of shop-floor workers in lean production. *Journal of Manufacturing Technology Management*, *27*(2), 287–311.

Wintersberger, D., & Muniz, J., Jr. (2017). Work organization and job design across national contexts. In D. Wintersberger (Ed.), *International human Resource management: A case study approach* (1 ed., Vol. 1, pp. 243–268). Kogan Page Publishers.

Yusof, E. M. M., Othman, M. S., & Yusof, A. R. M. (2018). Operational dashboard: Accelerator for shop floor workers. *International Journal of Engineering & Technology*, *7*(2.29), 4–6.

3 Managing Knowledge in China and Brazil

The changing landscape of international competition, accompanied by the rise of multinationals from emerging markets (Williamson & Zeng, 2009), has created a change in thinking among knowledge management scholars in favour of a particularistic approach of researching knowledge sharing (Hong et al., 2017). Brazil and China are two representatives in the BRICS (Brazil, Russian, India, China and South Africa) economies (Klafke et al., 2016), and they are considered as a relevant research context to examine the impact of context-specific cultural and institutional contextual conditions on knowledge sharing in production environments (Muniz et al., 2019; Tong & Mitra, 2009).

Cultural factors impacting on knowledge sharing may stem both from organizational (Gonzalez & Martins, 2014) and national culture (Ardichvili et al., 2006; Barachini, 2009; Gonzalez & Martins, 2014; Goswami et al., 2020). As organizational culture is influenced by national culture, we need to consider relevant cultural values in China and Brazil, which serve as the foundations for their knowledge sharing behaviours.

Chinese Cultural Values and Impact on Knowledge Sharing

Face

Face refers to the respect, pride and dignity generated by one's social achievements and practices (Leung & Chan, 2003). It can also be understood as a behavioural strategy or orientation to avoid negative evaluations and maintain social status in all potentially destructive situations (Keil et al., 2007). Although face issues are not unique to China, 'caring for one's face' is an important part of Chinese cultural values (Huang et al., 2008) driving their behavioural tendencies in work settings. When Chinese people encounter positive or negative comments, they will feel the pressures of gaining or losing face, respectively (Hwang, 2006).

Face-prone people tend to exhibit a strong desire for personal advantages and recognition from the public (Huang et al., 2011), which can be gained through

DOI: 10.4324/9781003112136-3

the recognition of others and the improvement of social status. Meanwhile, face-prone people try to avoid losing face in any situation. Losing face is an embarrassing situation that may lead to feelings of shame and humiliation (Kim & Nam, 1998; Zhang et al., 2011) and even causes disrespect among others (Huang et al., 2008). People lose face when they fail to meet the requirements or obligations associated with their social status (Keil et al., 2007). In order to protect themselves from losing face, Chinese people always adopt a proactive strategy to save and protect their face as much as possible.

Face gaining or saving affects the tendency of knowledge sharing. Face is a double-edged sword with both positive and negative effects (Huang et al., 2011). Overall speaking, those who care more about face-saving tend to be less willing to share knowledge with others, whereas people who need positive face (face gaining) tend to share knowledge. On the one hand, people with a high tendency for face gaining attach great importance to self-worthiness and social evaluation. They prefer to show their strengths and abilities in order to win recognition and admiration from others (Huang et al., 2011). As a result, they tend to maximize the value provided to the organization through knowledge sharing (Bock et al., 2005). The sense of competence and self-respect embodied in the knowledge sharing has a strong impact on their willingness to disclosure what they know with others (Ding et al., 2017). When provided with extrinsic rewards from the organization, employees with high face orientation may perceive such preferential treatment as a formal recognition of their abilities and efforts (Hau et al., 2013). In this case, their willingness to share knowledge increases. At the same time, employees with high face orientation are also very concerned about the perception of their colleagues (Huang et al., 2011). Knowledge sharing can be maintained under a reciprocal situation when both parties recognize and value the expertise of others. In this case, their willingness to share knowledge is further enhanced (Ding et al., 2017).

On the other hand, Chinese people who need positive face (face-saving) tend to be less willing to share knowledge. They tend to see themselves as closely connected to a social group, and any individual actions that might threaten the group's harmony are considered inappropriate (Markus & Kitayama, 1991; Willnat et al., 2002). Thus, people maintain cohesive social norms with a strong desire to 'blend in' with others (Earley, 1994). Failure to do so would result in a loss of face, not only for individuals but also for the collective.

Therefore, losing face also seriously endangers an individual's social status and relationships with others in the society, and every effort must be made to avoid such consequence (Lim, 1994). Under a fear of shame or humiliation, a high respect for tradition and an emphasis on quick success can be obstacles to knowledge management. The importance of face-saving for Chinese (Buckley et al., 2006; Ding et al., 2017) exert some emotional pressures on the knowledge seekers, thus implicating their social interactions with the knowledge contributors. Especially for those with higher hierarchical position, fear of losing their social standing and authority in front of their peers or subordinates might undermine their willingness to raise request for knowledge sharing (McAdam et al., 2012).

For the Chinese cultural tradition, the consequences of losing face are usually more serious than the consequences of not having face (Zhang et al., 2011), because doing so may result in loss of social status, thus forcing individuals not to engage in any behaviour that may threaten their image (Kam & Bond, 2008). In order to avoid losing face, those Chinese will try to conduct face protection activities as precautionary measures, such as not taking unnecessary risks and avoiding making mistakes in public (Huang et al., 2008). Ardichvili et al. (2006) found that Chinese employees are often unlikely to be stimulated to speak a lot in public and to stand out. Most employees feel rather comfortable asking questions and contributions to discussions in public, as long as these interactions contribute to improved job performance. People with a strong care for face-saving refrain from revealing their real feelings and thoughts during the process of sharing knowledge (Young, 2014). Furthermore, they are more likely to feel anxious when interacting with the superior due to the possible consequences of not being able to convey a positive impression to these people (Goffman, 1955). In fact, knowledge sharing requires individuals to interact with competent people and powerful figures (Young, 2014). Therefore, speaking in public risks exposing one's weaknesses in front of these important people, which may lead to public embarrassment (Young et al., 2012). The arguments above suggest that Chinese with face-saving concerns tend to avoid any negative evaluation from other people for maintaining their social status and self-esteem (Ding et al., 2017). In this way, face-saving weakens the reciprocal relationships and social interactions conducive for knowledge sharing.

Guanxi

As a special characteristic of Chinese culture, *guanxi* exists in social networks. For Chinese people, *guanxi* is not only a bond, but also a unique form of relationship (Xin & Pearce, 1996). 'Guanxi' (關系) in Chinese literally means 'door lock' and 'connection'. Therefore, *guanxi* refers to the interpersonal connections between two parties through various social contacts. This concept applies to all types of interpersonal relationships in Chinese society where the desired specific behaviours or activities between two people depend on the strengths of their *guanxi* (Hu, 2009). On top of that, relationships have additional implications for the transfer of power, social status and resources (Hackley & Dong, 2001). Since Chinese people are usually highly relationship-oriented, *guanxi* is regarded as an essential element of personal networks (Buckley et al., 2010).

Guanxi can provide insights into the foundations that enable the participants to seek mutual benefits by interacting harmoniously over a long period of time (Hu, 2009). As collectivists, Chinese tend to avoid opportunistic behaviours, because they attach great importance to maintain interpersonal relationships and avoid aggressive ways of cooperating with others. Prior studies have shown that the reduction of opportunism depends on the strong relationship in doing business in China (Wong et al., 2005).

In Chinese culture, intra-organizational ties (i.e. close *guanxi*) are more effective than inter-organizational ties (i.e. loose *guanxi*) in searching for and sharing personal knowledge (Qing, 2008). Close *guanxi* can be divided into individual level and collective level. The individual level of *guanxi* refers to the friendships, emotional bonds and relationships developed among colleagues. When the communication channel between organizations is underdeveloped, interpersonal network plays an important role in knowledge sharing (Weir & Hutchings, 2005). In other words, directional *guanxi* plays an important role in knowledge sharing intention. Chinese tends to maintain *guanxi* with people around them by treating them well and helping each other. All these activities help to promote the smooth progress and development of the *guanxi* (Huang et al., 2008). As for the collective level *of guanxi*, the focal person as the core beneficiary of inter-organizational relationships shares the responsibility to promote knowledge sharing (Gong, 2011). In a team environment, developing *guanxi* can help the individual to join the core group and elevate the social status from an outsider to an insider (Weir & Hutchings, 2005). Members of the core team are expected to contribute and share their valuable knowledge (Hutchings & Murray, 2002).

Loose *guanxi* also exists at both individual level and collective level. While the former is found to improve the employees' willingness to participate in knowledge sharing driven by a high level of trust, communication and commitment (Zhao & Anand, 2009; Park & Luo, 2001; Ramasamy et al., 2006), new employees assigned to key positions are likely to be supported by other colleagues with good *guanxi* (Cohen & Levinthal, 1990). The team's ability to maintain good individual *guanxi* will mitigate the negative impact of high personnel turnover on knowledge sharing (Davison & Ou, 2008; Uzzi & Spiro, 1997). Moreover, loose guanxi at collective level can nurture an organizational environment conducive for the acquisition and transfer of knowledge (Walsh & Ungson, 1991). As a result, *guanxi* at the collective level and individual level complement each other for knowledge sharing.

Collectivism

Individualism and collectivism represent two cultural value dimensions underpinning how individuals in different countries perceive their relationship with others (Hofstede, 1980). Some countries are more individualistic, such as the United States, while others are more collectivistic, such as China. Individualism is composed of loosely connected individuals who believe that they are independent of the collective and are motivated by their own preferences and needs. They tend to emphasize individual needs rather than group needs and are more competitive (Wagner, 1995).

However, collectivism is composed of closely connected individuals who believe that they belong to one or more social and cultural communities (e.g., family, colleagues and friends) and are motivated by corresponding norms and obligations imposed upon them. People from collectivistic cultures show a greater tendency to cooperate (Wagner, 1995) and prioritize the team goals over their own interests (Triandis, 1994). House et al. (2004) defined collectivism as the degree to which individuals express loyalty, pride and cohesion in their families or organizations. Individuals in a collectivist society believe that they are interdependent with other members in the group, care about the impacts of their own behaviour and are more likely to sacrifice their own personal interests for greater good (Issac & Baral, 2019).

Individuals with individualism or collectivism share knowledge under different incentives (Triandis & Gelfand, 1998). Accordingly, individualistic culture tends to protect their own interests and well-being, thus weakening the willingness of knowledge sharing (Yu, 2014). They believe their own 'self' is independent of the surrounding social environment (Bhagat et al., 2002), so they tend to work alone and have less opportunities of knowledge sharing. The lack of knowledge sharing will also have a negative impact on the process of knowledge externalization and internalization (Ray, 2014).

However, for collectivistic culture, such as Chinese, organizational members are more likely to share organizational goals and collective beliefs. In this case, when they share knowledge, they are doing it for the benefits of the organization as they believe that collective interests are more important (Qin et al., 2011). Collectivistic culture has a positive impact on people's knowledge sharing attitude (Hwang & Kim, 2007), while individualistic culture has no significant effect on knowledge sharing attitude (Fathi et al., 2011). As a result, people from highly individualistic cultures have lower knowledge sharing tendency within their working groups than people in the collectivist cultures (Ray, 2014). In case of conflicts between collective interests and self-interests, people from collectivistic culture are more willing to share knowledge than those in individualistic culture (Yu, 2014).

In order to better understand how the flows of communication affect knowledge sharing, scholars associate individualism/collectivism with horizontal/vertical dimensions (Bhagat et al., 2002). When these two dimensions are superimposed on the dimensions of individualism/collectivism, a clearer picture emerges regarding how information and knowledge are transferred and processed by different social members (Triandis et al., 1995). Horizontal collectivism refers to the integration of individuals and people in the inner group. Vertical collectivism indicates the likelihood of individuals within the inner group to think differently. Horizontal individualism signifies an autonomous self, but the individual is more or less equal in status compared with others. Vertical individualism construes that people are relatively unique and have unequal status (Bhagat et al., 2002).

While collectivism facilitates trust and knowledge sharing with 'in-group' members, there is usually scepticism towards 'outsiders'. Therefore, China remains a challenging setting for encouraging knowledge sharing amongst the workforce (Chen & Hung, 2010; Huang et al., 2008; Jolly, 2002; Ma et al., 2014; McAdam et al., 2012; Tong & Mitra, 2009). First, the strong emphasis on particularistic and intense social relationships (Weir & Hutchings, 2005) among

Chinese workers may hinder the knowledge sharing processes. Specifically, Chinese people are found to be hesitant to share valuable information to other employees who are considered not as part of the 'in-group' members, as revealed, for example, in a comparison between manager views in Australian and Taiwanese-owned firms (Chow et al., 1999). Due to their seemingly low trust towards outsiders and a fear of potential loss of individual gains (Ding et al., 2017), it is seen as inconceivable for the Chinese to devote considerable time for converting privately held tacit knowledge into public domains that can be accessible by everyone in organizations.

Although collectivists are more willing to share knowledge (Chow et al., 2000), they only communicate with other members in the inner group, and these members may be few in the organization. But for people with horizontal collectivism, they interact freely with anyone in the organization (Bhagat et al., 2002). Hence, when there are differences in one (e.g., vertical individualism and vertical collectivism) or more dimensions (e.g., vertical individualism and horizontal collectivism), knowledge sharing becomes more difficult (Bhagat et al., 2002). People with a high degree of collectivism will not engage in knowledge hiding due to their dependence on others (Issac & Baral, 2019). However, vertical individualists tend to emphasize transfer of explicit knowledge and are relatively independent (Bhagat et al., 2002). Therefore, both horizontal and vertical collectivism have different impacts on knowledge sharing behaviour (Sandhu & Ching, 2014).

Trust

Trust exists when one party has a positive expectation towards other's behaviours, shaped by integrity, honesty, goodwill and reliability (Ellonen et al., 2008), and the favourable impact on their own interests (Mayer et al., 1995). Interpersonal trust is about the evaluation of the credibility of specific people (such as managers and colleagues). Lack of trust has thus been shown to have a negative impact on a variety of organizational phenomena, including job satisfaction, stress, organizational commitment, productivity and knowledge sharing (Bechky, 2003; Davenport et al., 1998; Kramer, 1999; Levin & Cross, 2004; Tagliaventi & Mattarelli, 2006).

At the national level, cultural differences between countries affect the formation of trust among in-group members and out-group members (Triandis et al., 1995). Prior studies showed that collectivists trust their in-group members more, whereas individualists behave in an opposite way (Huff & Kelley, 2005). In countries with a high culture of trust, such as United States and Germany (Fukuyama, 1995), enterprises have the advantage to develop close relationship with other trading partners. However, in countries or regions with low trust culture, such as China, Hong Kong and Taiwan (Fukuyama, 1995), companies have a strong atmosphere of trust for small organizations (Huff & Kelley, 2005). For a low trust society, the distrust of outsiders is inherent in their behaviours, which inhibit the development of external relationship with customers (Triandis et al., 1995). When compared with their counterparts, low trust countries from collectivist cultures cooperate more with their compatriots in foreign territories than with foreigners (Chen & Li, 2005). This may partly explain why, except for Japan, few companies from Asia can become world-class marketers to develop global brands and organizations on a global scale (Huff & Kelley, 2005).

At the enterprise level, the key to cooperation and knowledge sharing is mutual trust (Foss et al., 2009). Employees working in a team-oriented culture do not regard other employees (or employees of other projects) as competitors. They trust other colleagues and need not to worry about knowledge leaking (Shao et al., 2015). As a result, employees will not mind to take the risk of sharing knowledge across teams. This interpersonal trust allows employees to see others as friends and family, so they are more likely to communicate with each other. When a group of people is working together, they will share stories and experiences by telling each other how to carry out their work (Ke & Wei, 2008; Mueller, 2012). This is conducive for skills development (Wiewiora et al., 2013). Therefore, improving knowledge sharing in the workplace relies on interpersonal trust (Abrams et al., 2003; Mayer et al., 1995), since this will increase the overall knowledge exchange and the likelihood of absorbing and understanding the knowledge acquired (Abrams et al., 2003; Levin & Cross, 2004).

In addition, gaining the trust of top management can also facilitate knowledge sharing among project teams (Mueller, 2012). With the confidence from top management about the competence of employees to carry out their tasks effectively, they are more willing to participate in sharing their knowledge with others during the work process even though not being required (Mueller, 2012). At the same time, top managers attach great importance to such sharing of best practices for avoiding mistakes, because it can improve the quality of project team achievements. The improvement of employee satisfaction can be obtained from the reduction of workload through knowledge sharing.

By embedding the importance of teamwork into its corporate culture (Mueller, 2012), employees are encouraged to participate in social interactions and interpersonal communication. People sharing the team culture tend to focus on a sense of belonging and trust, thereby encouraging other employees to complete tasks on a collective basis (Cameron & Quinn, 2011). All these factors contribute to knowledge sharing among team members. Therefore, it is not only employees' trust on other colleagues that promotes knowledge sharing (Levin & Cross, 2004; Renzl, 2008; Von Krogh, 1998), but also senior managers' trust on employees and corporate culture.

Brazilian Cultural Values and Impact on Knowledge Sharing

Brazil has faced cycles of growth and development throughout history in context of challenges related to socio-economic issues, political changes, regional inequalities and population diversity (Baer, 2008). Brazil was officially colonized by the Portuguese and had a strong African and indigenous influence during its colonization, and historical migratory processes brought influence from France, Germany, Italy, Japan, among others (Alcadipani & Crubellate, 2003) who were located in different regions and producing different cultural characteristics within the country (Motta & Gomes, 2021).

The indigenous context indicates that Brazilian networks may be viewed as positive personal relationships based on cooperation, mutual support and trust that can increase flexibility through gathering and disseminating knowledge and relocating different types of resources in unpredictable and changing environments (Park et al., 2018), which is beneficial for knowledge sharing within companies.

Brazilian society has cultural traits that influence its social practices and, in particular, the organizational culture (Araujo et al., 2014; Pereira et al., 2013). The Brazilian cultural traits are grounded in Brazilian colonialism (Araujo et al., 2014) and the knowledge management in production systems may be related to three cultural traits as below:

- Brazilian way (*jeitinho*) refers to creative ingenuity in achieving short-term solutions to the challenges of everyday life, which include bureaucratic issues that arise in hierarchical contexts.
- Formalism describes the gap that exists in Brazil between prescriptive written norms and current behaviours, and cannot be understood simply as a preference for written rules.
- Personalism explains how Brazilians use their social networks to resolve problems.

The ambiguity in formal procedures (formalism), the excess of improvisation and the use of short-term solutions (Brazilian way) and the need to rely on personal relationships to resolve problems (personalism) represent cultural traits faced by the Brazilian companies and their employees (Araujo et al., 2014), which influence the knowledge sharing practices.

Brazilian Jeitinho

The Brazilian way (*jeitinho Brasileiro*) is a social mechanism widely used in Brazilian society as a problem-solving strategy and entails bending or breaking the rules in order to deal with difficult or forbidding situations (Amado & Brasil, 1991). The whole idea of *jeitinho* entails a relationship of trust among the people involved (Duarte, 2006) for creating a rapid, improvised and creative response to a law, rule or custom that on its surface prevents someone from doing something (Page, 1995).

Brazilian way is a useful and yet informal strategy to 'get things done' in work organizations (Duarte, 2006), which allows excessive formalism to be bypassed in practice, thus alleviating pressures and emphasizing the importance of personal relationships (Hilal, 2006). It has similarities with *guanxi* orientation as both concepts involve social interactions based on reciprocity and trust between people who know each other. They are important elements of cultural identity largely premised on networks of reciprocity and entail a relationship of trust between the people (Park et al., 2018), which are essential elements to facilitate knowledge sharing.

The Brazilian way indicates a creative way to quickly bring short-term solutions to problems and may include ways to circumvent bureaucratic rules or to deal with problems with superiors in a rigid and strongly hierarchical management, aiming for equality and reciprocity (Rodriguez, 2020; Teixeira et al., 2019; Torres et al., 2015). This may support knowledge sharing (Chen & Hung, 2010; Ellonen et al., 2008; Huff & Kelley, 2005; Ma et al., 2014).

Brazilian *jeitinho* looks as a transgressive practice in relationships based on a stronger sense of formality (Park et al., 2018). The Brazilian way has a duality perceived as similar to the use of favours and as a very positive way of dealing with a difficult situation or a harmless problem-solving strategy. Nevertheless, it also has a negative connotation in some cases related to a notion of corruption when more selfishly in search for personal benefits (Amado & Brasil, 1991; Park et al., 2018). Its application is defined by satisfying the parties involved and must leave neither partly feeling used nor manipulated (Araujo et al., 2014).

The role of Brazilian *jeitinho* in management can be observed in its dealing with restrictions and bureaucracy by responding to the severe and prohibitive Brazilian legal environment with high level of bureaucratization. Besides, it can also facilitate the relationship between customers and suppliers, making operational rules more flexible or by customizing general practices for specific partners and dealing with issues related to intra-organizational processes (Park et al., 2018), such as continuous improvement in organizations.

The knowledge management-friendly culture is related to relational orientation and the high in-group collectivism of the Brazilian culture, and the team-oriented and participative leadership often practiced in Brazilian organizations (Dávila et al., 2019). There is a positive influence between Brazilian way and knowledge sharing, and it is largely driven by interpersonal relationships, trust, the feelings of kindness and concerns for other individuals. Interpersonal relationships are important for professional career development, while people must relate harmoniously in the work context and they may strive to achieve a good relationship with their colleagues and managers.

Formalism

Formalism is a very common cultural trait in Brazil, especially when it comes to laws and their enforcements, which involve reducing risks, ambiguity and uncertainty by creating rules, regulations and procedures (Araujo et al., 2014; Pereira et al., 2013). The rigid regulations, the gaps between technical rules and the day-to-day implementation of regulations have its origins in colonialism from Portugal (Araujo et al., 2014), which implements laws distant from the country's reality. Formalism represents a tacit way of accepting norms and rules, but adapting them to the context, which often represents a discrepancy between conduct and prescribed norms (Pereira et al., 2013). The Brazilian way reacts to the excessive formalism and rigid governmental bureaucracy inherited from the Portuguese colonial administration, which is still present today in Brazilian society (Park et al., 2018).

Formalism refers to the degree of labour codification and the rules that exist in an organization, and centralization is related to the authority of decision-making that is delegated to the lower levels in the organization. To create a favourable context of worker knowledge sharing, it is not enough to define the tasks of each worker and to establish a low level of formalism or a low level of protocol communications (Chión et al., 2020). Continuous improvement processes based on low-protocol communication and decentralized decisions (i.e. *kaizen*, problem solving activities) may support the worker engagement in this context (Chió et al., 2020; Muniz et al., 2019; Muniz, Ribeiro, et al., 2021). Delbridge et al. (2010) indicate that blue-collar workers contribute with 'contextual' knowledge and 'conventional' wisdom to the problem-solving process, and Muniz et al. (2019) highlight that workers' communication for tacit knowledge socialization on the shop floor through dialogue, observation, imitation and practice is relevant in Brazil and China.

Hierarchy in Brazilian culture expresses the tendency to centralize power, creating social distance in relationships between different social groups and passivity and acceptance of less favoured groups (Pereira et al., 2013). The hierarchy and formalism created thereafter bring constraints to continuous improvement processes, which need employees to discuss the solutions (socialization), supported by trust and knowledge sharing. Dávila et al. (2019) indicate that managers of Brazilian organizations are transforming their organizational structures to become more flexible and innovative.

Personalism

Personalism refers to the importance given by Brazilians to the relationships established between people, families, friends and co-workers, so this trait is characterized by a complex set of intermediations that privilege individuals according to the criteria that define their relationships (Pereira et al., 2013).

Paternalistic leadership style, which is associated with personalism, leading to the confusion between the public and private instances of the individual and therefore his/her management, is based more on the loyalty and docility to the leadership (a particular form of favouritism) rather than professionalism. The existence of an abyss of power among the professional segments of an organization associated with personalism leads to a rigid formalism of structures, which generates the hierarchy and standardization of procedures (Moreira & Rocha, 2018).

Brazilian society has a strong emphasis on personal relationships that guide individual and collective behaviour. Such relationships are the result of feelings of affection, respect, trust, cordiality and consideration that bring one person closer to another, forming an intimate social network that subordinates and conditions the individual and influences their knowledge sharing (Borges et al., 2019). The Brazilians value the interests of the group higher than individual interests by creating trust and commitment among workers that facilitate informal interactions among workers to support knowledge sharing (Dávila et al., 2019).

Personalism indicates the extent of which rules can be interpreted more loosely based on the specificity of a situation and the nature of relationships with the people involved. China and Brazil have collectivistic cultures that look for contextual cues in information and tend to disregard information in writing (Ardichvili et al., 2006), which is supported by socialization among employees to achieve objectives, and through interpersonal interactions due to their unstructured and experience-based characteristics (Borges et al., 2019; Muniz et al., 2019; Nakano et al., 2013).

Based on the Hofstede's research, the essential characteristics of the Brazilian style of management are high power distance, collectivistic behaviours, high need to avoid uncertainties, feminine value orientation, low-performance orientation and short term orientation (Moreira & Rocha, 2018; Motta & Gomes, 2021). In Brazilian context, knowledge sharing strengthens the relationships among employees, contributes to the integration with other members of the organization, engages new members of the organization and promotes cooperation between members with a common interest. There is a strong concern among Brazilians to make one's words clear, and they have a stronger preference for face-to-face communication (Ardichvili et al., 2006; Muniz et al., 2019; Muniz, Wintersberger, et al., 2021).

In Brazil, the issue of modesty is not as important as in China. Brazilian employees are enthusiastic for sharing information and knowledge with others in their organization and are willing to ask questions and provide answers more often without the concern for being perceived as immodest (Ardichvili et al., 2006; Muniz et al., 2019). The in-group and out-group distinction could be a barrier of knowledge sharing from the Brazilian employees' standpoint when dealing with other employees (Ardichvili et al., 2006). Besides, Brazilians tend to see their relationships with other business people as interpersonal in nature and place a high value on these relationships (Dávila et al., 2019; Muniz et al., 2019).

The differences between Chinese and Brazilian workers' perceived importance attributed to knowledge sharing processes reinforce our understanding about the challenges of knowledge sharing across cultures (Hong et al., 2006; Muniz et al., 2019) and lends support to a more particularistic debate of knowledge management (Glisby & Holden, 2003). While automotive workers in Brazil like to engage in more dialogues among workers and training as relevant to support knowledge sharing, Chinese workers prefer formal learning based on standard operation procedures (Muniz et al., 2019). This may serve as a strong reminder for 'bringing the culture back' when researching knowledge sharing in organizations (Ipe, 2003).

As a conclusion, the three Brazilian cultural traits (*jeitinho*, formalism and personalism) are interrelated and they create a context for promoting the sharing of knowledge among employees. Brazilians consider many official regulations far from the reality of the country, contributing to the adoption of formalism. The inadequacy of regulations creates the need to adopt creative practices to solve everyday problems (Brazilian *jeitinho*). Since individuals can often be in a position to apply the Brazilian *jeitinho*, which cannot be implemented indiscriminately in all situations, personalism emerges as a criterion for defining which individuals can receive this 'transgressive' benefit. The combination of these cultural traits creates a social scenario supported by hierarchy and cordiality (Araujo et al., 2014), which influence knowledge sharing on the organizations.

References

Abrams, L. C., Cross, R., Lesser, E., & Levin, D. Z. (2003). Nurturing interpersonal trust in knowledge-sharing networks. *Academy of Management Perspectives, 17*(4), 64–77.

Alcadipani, R., & Crubellate, J. M. (2003). Cultura organizacional: generalizações improváveis e conceituações imprecisas (Portuguese). *Revista de Administração de Empresas, 43*(2), 64–77.

Amado, G., & Brasil, H. H. (1991). Organizational behaviors and cultural context: The Brazilian *jeitinho*. *International Studies of Management & Organization, 21*(3), 38–61.

Araujo, B. F. B., Teixeira, M. L. M., Cruz, P. B., & Malini, E. (2014). Understanding the adaptation of organisational and self-initiated expatriates in the context of Brazilian culture. *International Journal of Human Resource Management, 25*(18), 2489–2509.

Ardichvili, A., Maurer, M., Li, W., Wentling, T., & Stuedemann, R. (2006). Cultural influences on knowledge sharing through online communities of practice. *Journal of Knowledge Management, 10*(1), 94–107.

Baer, W. (2008). *The Brazilian economy: Growth and development* (6th ed.). Lynne Rienner.

Barachini, F. (2009). Cultural and social issues for knowledge sharing. *Journal of Knowledge Management, 13*(1), 98–110.

Bechky, B. A. (2003). Sharing meaning across occupational communities: The transformation of understanding on a production floor. *Organization Science, 14*(3), 312–330.

Bhagat, R. S., Kedia, B., Englis, P., & Triandis, H. (2002). Cultural variations in the cross-border transfer of organizational knowledge: An integrative framework. *Academy of Management Review, 27*(2), 204–221.

Bock, G. W., Zmud, R. W., Kim, Y. G., & Lee, J. N. (2005). Behavioral intention formation in knowledge sharing: Examining the roles of extrinsic motivators, social-psychological forces, and organizational climate. *MIS Quarterly, 29*(1), 87–111.

Borges, R., Bernardi, M., & Petrin, R. (2019). Cross-country findings on tacit knowledge sharing: Evidence from the Brazilian and Indonesian IT workers. *Journal of Knowledge Management, 23*(4), 742–762.

Buckley, P. J., Clegg, J., & Tan, H. (2010). Cultural awareness in knowledge transfer to China: The role of *guanxi* and *mianzi*. *Journal of World Business, 41*(3), 275–288.

Buckley, P. J., Clegg, J., & Wang, C. (2006). Inward FDI and host country productivity: Evidence from China's electronics industry. *Transnational Corporations, 15*(1), 13–37.

Cameron, K. S., & Quinn, R. E. (2011). *Diagnosing and changing organizational culture*. John Wiley & Sons.

Chen, C. J., & Hung, S. W. (2010). To give or to receive? Factors influencing members' knowledge sharing and community promotion in professional virtual communities. *Information & Management, 47*(4), 226–236.

Chen, X. P., & Li, S. (2005). Cross-national differences in cooperative decision-making in mixed-motive business contexts: The mediating effect of vertical and horizontal individualism. *Journal of International Business Studies*, *36*(6), 622–636.

Chión, S. J., Charles, V., & Morales, J. (2020). The impact of organisational culture, organisational structure and technological infrastructure on process improvement through knowledge sharing. *Business Process Management Journal*, *26*(6), 1443–1472.

Chow, C. W., Deng, F. J., & Ho, J. L. (2000). The openness of knowledge sharing within organizations: A comparative study of the United States and the People's Republic of China. *Journal of Management Accounting Research*, *12*(1), 65–95.

Chow, C. W., Shields, M. D., & Wu, A. (1999). The importance of national culture in the design of and preference for management controls for multi-national operations. *Accounting, Organizations and Society*, *24*(5–6), 441–461.

Cohen, W. M., & Levinthal, D. A. (1990). Absorptive capacity: A new perspective on learning and innovation. *Administrative Science Quarterly*, *35*(1), 128–152.

Davenport, S., Davies, J., & Grimes, C. (1998). Collaborative research programmes: Building trust from difference. *Technovation*, *19*(1), 31–40.

Dávila, G. A., Andreeva, T., & Varvakis, G. (2019). Knowledge management in Brazil: What governance mechanisms are needed to boost innovation? *Management and Organization Review*, *15*(4), 857–886.

Davison, R. M., & Ou, C. X. (2008). *Guanxi*, knowledge and online intermediaries in China. *Chinese Management Studies*, *2*(4), 281–302.

Delbridge, R., Lowe, J., & Oliver, N. (2010). Shop floor responsibilities under lean teamwork. *Human Relations*, *53*(11), 1459–1479. http://dx.doi.org/10.1177/00187267005311003

Ding, G., Liu, H., Huang, Q., & Gu, J. (2017). Moderating effects of *guanxi* and face on the relationship between psychological motivation and knowledge-sharing in china. *Journal of Knowledge Management*, *21*(5), 1077–1097.

Duarte, F. (2006). Exploring the interpersonal transaction of the Brazilian *jeitinho* in bureaucratic contexts. *Organization*, *13*(4), 509–527.

Earley, P. C. (1994). Self or group? Cultural effects of training on self-efficacy and performance. *Administrative Science Quarterly*, *39*(1), 89–117.

Ellonen, R., Blomqvist, K., & Puumalainen, K. (2008). The role of trust in organizational innovativeness. *Journal of Innovation Management*, *11*(2), 160–181.

Fathi, M., Cyril, E. U., & Goh, G. (2011). Key determinants of knowledge sharing in an electronics manufacturing firm in Malaysia. *Library Review*, *60*(1), 53–67.

Foss, N. J., Minbaeva, D. B., Pedersen, T., & Reinholt, M. (2009). Encouraging knowledge sharing among employees: How job design matters. *Human Resource Management*, *48*(6), 871–893.

Fukuyama, F. (1995). *Trust: The social virtues and the creation of prosperity*. Free Press.

Glisby, M., & Holden, N. (2003). Contextual constraints in knowledge management theory: The cultural embeddedness of Nonaka's knowledge-creating company. *Knowledge and Process Management*, *10*(1), 29–36.

Goffman, E. (1955). On face-work: An analysis of ritual elements in social interaction. *Psychiatry*, *18*(3), 213–231.

Gong, B. (2011). Individual and collective inter organizational *guanxi*: The dynamics of *guanxi* and knowledge sharing. *Frontiers of Business Research in China*, *5*(4), 473–489.

Gonzalez, R. V. D., & Martins, M. F. (2014). Mapping the organizational factors that support knowledge management in the Brazilian automotive industry. *Journal of Knowledge Management*, *18*(1), 152–176.

Goswami, A. K., Agrawal, R. K., & Goswami, M. (2020). Influence of national culture on knowledge management process: Literature review and research agenda. *Benchmarking: An International Journal, 28*(4), 1186–1212.

Hackley, C. A., & Dong, Q. (2001). American public relations networking encounters China's *guanxi*. *Public Relations Quarterly, 46*(2), 16–19.

Hau, Y. S., Kim, B., Lee, H., & Kim, Y. G. (2013). The effects of individual motivations and social capital on employees' tacit and explicit knowledge sharing intentions. *International Journal of Information Management, 33*(2), 356–366.

Hilal, A. (2006). Brazilian national culture, organizational culture and cultural agreement: Findings from a multinational company. *International Journal of Cross Cultural Management, 6*(2), 139–167.

Hofstede, G. (1980). *Culture's consequences: International differences in work-related values.* Sage Publications.

Hong, J., Snell, R., & Easterby-Smith, M. (2006). Cross-cultural influences of organizational learning in MNCs: The case of Japanese companies in China. *Journal of International Management, 12*(4), 408–429.

Hong, J., Snell, R., & Rowley, C. (2017). Asia pacific as a research context for organizational learning: Background and research directions. *Asia Pacific Business Review, 23*(4), 467–474.

House, R. J., Hanges, P. J., Javidan, M., Dorfman, P. W., & Gupta, V. (Eds.). (2004). *Culture, leadership and organizations: The GLOBE study of 62 societies.* Sage Publications.

Hu, M. L. M. (2009). Knowledge sharing and innovative service behavior relationship: Guanxi as mediator. *Social Behavior and Personality: An International Journal, 37*(7), 977–992.

Huang, Q., Davison, R. M., & Gu, J. (2008). Impact of personal and cultural factors on knowledge sharing in China. *Asia Pacific Journal of Management, 25*(3), 451–471.

Huang, Q., Davison, R. M., & Gu, J. (2011). The impact of trust, guanxi orientation and face on the intention of Chinese employees and managers to engage in peer-to-peer tacit and explicit knowledge sharing. *Information Systems Journal, 21*(6), 557–577.

Huff, L., & Kelley, L. (2005). Is collectivism a liability? The impact of culture on organizational trust and customer orientation: A seven-nation study. *Journal of Business Research, 58*(1), 96–102.

Hutchings, K., & Murray, G. (2002). Working with *guanxi*: An assessment of the implications of globalization on business networking in China. *Creativity and Innovation Management, 11*(3), 184–191.

Hwang, K. K. (2006). Moral face and social face: Contingent self-esteem in Confucian society. *International Journal of Psychology, 41*(4), 276–281.

Hwang, Y., & Kim, D. J. (2007). Understanding affective commitment, collectivist culture, and social influence in relation to knowledge sharing in technology mediated learning. *IEEE Transactions on Professional Communications, 50*(3), 232–248.

Ipe, M. (2003). Knowledge sharing in organizations: A conceptual framework. *Human Resource Development Review, 2*(4), 337–359.

Issac, A. C., & Baral, R. (2019). Knowledge hiding in two contrasting cultural contexts. *VINE Journal of Information and Knowledge Management Systems, 50*(3), 455–475.

Jolly, D. (2002). Sharing knowledge and decision power in Sino-foreign joint ventures. *Asia Pacific Business Review, 9*(2), 81–100.

Kam, C. C. S., & Bond, M. H. (2008). Role of emotions and behavioural responses in mediating the impact of face loss on relationship deterioration: Are Chinese more face-sensitive than Americans? *Asian Journal of Social Psychology, 11*(2), 175–184.

Ke, W., & Wei, K. K. (2008). Organizational culture and leadership in ERP implementation. *Decision Support Systems, 45*(2), 208–218.

Keil, M., Im, G. P., & Mähring, M. (2007). Reporting bad news on software projects: The effects of culturally constituted views of face-saving. *Information Systems Journal, 17*(1), 59–87.

Kim, J. Y., & Nam, S. H. (1998). The concept and dynamics of face: Implications for organizational behavior in Asia. *Organization Science, 9*(4), 522–534.

Klafke, R. V., Lievore, C., Picinin, C. T., de Francisco, A. C., & Pilatti, L. A. (2016). Primary knowledge management practices applied in Brazil, Russia, India and China (BRIC) industries from 2001–2010. *Journal of Knowledge Management, 20*(4), 812–828.

Kramer, R. M. (1999). Trust and distrust in organizations: Emerging perspectives, enduring questions. *Annual Review of Psychology, 50*(1), 569–598.

Leung, T. K., & Chan, R. Y. K. (2003). Face, favour and positioning-a Chinese power game. *European Journal of Marketing, 37*(11–12), 1575–1598.

Levin, D. Z., & Cross, R. (2004). The strength of weak ties you can trust: The mediating role of trust in effective knowledge transfer. *Management Science, 50*(11), 1477–1490.

Lim, T. S. (1994). Facework and interpersonal relationships. In S. Ting-Toomey (Ed.), *The challenge of facework: Cross-cultural and interpersonal issues* (pp. 209–229). SUNY Press.

Markus, H. R., & Kitayama, S. (1991). Culture and the self: Implications for cognition, emotion, and motivation. *Psychological Review, 98*(2), 224.

Mayer, R. C., Davis, J. H., & Schoorman, F. D. (1995). An integrative model of organizational trust. *Academy of Management Review, 20*(3), 709–734.

McAdam, R., Moffett, S., & Peng, J. (2012). Knowledge sharing in Chinese service organizations: A multi case cultural perspective. *Journal of Knowledge Management, 16*(1), 129–147.

Moreira, A. M. A., & Rocha, M. Z. B. (2018). To understand the "Brazilian way" of school management: How national culture influences the organizational culture and school leadership. *Education Sciences, 8*(2), 88.

Motta, L. A. S., & Gomes, J. S. (2021). The characteristics from the national culture and its influence at the organizational subcultures: An analysis from Brazilian public management. *Public Organization Review, 22*(5), 1–19.

Mueller, J. (2012). Knowledge sharing between project teams and its cultural antecedents. *Journal of Knowledge Management, 16*(3), 435–447.

Muniz, J., Jr., Hong, J., Oliveira, S., Wintersberger, D., & Popadiuk, S. (2019). Knowledge sharing in the automotive sector: A comparative study of Chinese and Brazilian firms. *Production, 29*, 1–21.

Muniz, J., Jr., Ribeiro, V. B., & Pradhan, N. (2021). Knowledge-based assessment applied to lean Brazilian Toyota plants: Employees' perceptions. *International Journal of Knowledge Management, 17*(2), 1–22.

Muniz, J., Jr., Wintersberger, D., & Hong, J. L. (2021). Worker and manager judgments about factors that facilitate knowledge-sharing: Insights from a Brazilian automotive assembly line. *Knowledge and Process Management* (early view). doi: 10.1002/kpm.1693

Nakano, D., Muniz, J., Jr., & Batista, E. D. (2013). Engaging environments: Tacit knowledge sharing on the shop floor. *Journal of Knowledge Management, 17*(2), 290–306.

Page, J. A. (1995). *The Brazilians*. Addison-Wiley.

Park, S. H., & Luo, Y. (2001). Guanxi and organizational dynamics: Organizational networking in Chinese firms. *Strategic Management Journal, 22*(5), 455–477.

Park, C. L., Nunes, M. F., Muratbekova-Touron, M., & Moatti, V. (2018). The duality of the Brazilian jeitinho: An empirical investigation and conceptual framework. *Critical Perspectives on International Business*, *14*(4), 404–425.

Pereira, J. R., Cançado, A. C., Rodrigues, F. O., & Silva, E. E. (2013). Cultura organizacional e cultura brasileira: compreendendo as fragilidades do cooperativismo brasileiro. *NAU Social*, *4*(6), 61–81.

Qin, C., Ramburuth, P., & Wang, Y. (2011). A conceptual model of cultural distance, MNC subsidiary roles, and knowledge transfer in China-based subsidiaries. *Organizations and Markets in Emerging Economies*, *2*(2), 8–27.

Ramasamy, B., Goh, K. W., & Yeung, M. C. (2006). Is guanxi (relationship) a bridge to knowledge transfer? *Journal of Business Research*, *59*(1), 130–139.

Ray, D. (2014). Overcoming cross-cultural barriers to knowledge management using social media. *Journal of Enterprise Information Management*, *27*(1), 45–55.

Renzl, B. (2008). Trust in management and knowledge sharing: The mediating effects of fear and knowledge documentation. *Omega*, *36*(2), 206–220.

Sandhu, M. S., & Ching, P. W. (2014). Relationship between individual cultural values and knowledge sharing in selected multinational companies in Malaysia. *International Journal of Business and Economics*, *13*(1), 1–24.

Shao, Z., Wang, T., & Feng, Y. (2015). Impact of organizational culture and computer self-efficacy on knowledge sharing. *Industrial Management & Data Systems*, *27*(1), 45–55.

Tagliaventi, M. R., & Mattarelli, E. (2006). The role of networks of practice, value sharing, and operational proximity in knowledge flows between professional groups. *Human Relations*, *59*(3), 291–319.

Teixeira, E. K., Oliveira, M., & Curado, C. M. M. (2019). Pursuing innovation through knowledge sharing: Brazil and Portugal. *International Journal of Knowledge Management (IJKM)*, *15*(1), 69–84.

Tong, J., & Mitra, A. (2009). Chinese cultural influences on knowledge management practice. *Journal of Knowledge Management*, *13*(2), 49–62.

Torres, C. V., Alfinito, S., Galvão, C. A. D. S. P., & Tse, B. C. Y. (2015). Brazilian jeitinho versus Chinese guanxi: Investigating their informal influence on international business. *RAM. Revista de Administração Mackenzie*, *16*, 77–99.

Triandis, H. C. (1994). *Culture and social behavior*. McGraw Hill.

Triandis, H. C., Chan, D. K. S., Bhawuk, D. P., Iwao, S., & Sinha, J. B. (1995). Multimethod probes of allocentrism and idiocentrism. *International Journal of Psychology*, *30*(4), 461–480.

Triandis, H. C., & Gelfand, M. J. (1998). Converging measurement of horizontal and vertical individualism and collectivism. *Journal of Personality and Social Psychology*, *74*(1), 118–128.

Uzzi, B., & Spiro, J. (1997). Collaboration and creativity: The small world problem. *American Journal of Sociology*, *111*(2), 447–504.

Von Krogh, G. (1998). Care in knowledge creation. *California Management Review*, *40*(3), 133–153.

Wagner, J. A., III. (1995). Studies of individualism-collectivism: Effects on cooperation in groups. *Academy of Management Journal*, *38*(1), 152–173.

Walsh, J. P., & Ungson, G. R. (1991). Organizational memory. *Academy of Management Review*, *16*(1), 57–91.

Weir, D., & Hutchings, K. (2005). Cultural embeddedness and contextual constraints: Knowledge sharing in Chinese and Arab cultures. *Knowledge and Process Management*, *12*(2), 89–98.

Wiewiora, A., Trigunarsyah, B., Murphy, G., & Coffey, V. (2013). Organizational culture and willingness to share knowledge: A competing values perspective in Australian context. *International Journal of Project Management*, *31*(8), 1163–1174.

Williamson, P., & Zeng, M. (2009). *Chinese multinationals: Emerging through new global gateways*. In R. Ramamurti, & J. Singh (Eds.), *Emerging multinationals in emerging markets* (pp. 81–109). Cambridge University Press.

Willnat, L., Lee, W., & Detenber, B. H. (2002). Individual-level predictors of public outspokenness: A test of the spiral of silence theory in Singapore. *International Journal of Public Opinion Research*, *14*(4), 391–412.

Wong, A., Tjosvold, D., & Yu, Z. Y. (2005). Organizational partnerships in China: Self-interest, goal interdependence, and opportunism. *Journal of Applied Psychology*, *90*(4), 782–791.

Xin, K. K., & Pearce, J. L. (1996). *Guanxi*: Connections as substitutes for formal institutional support. *Academy of Management Journal*, *39*(6), 1641–1658.

Young, M. L. (2014). The formation of concern for face and its impact on knowledge sharing intention in knowledge management systems. *Knowledge Management Research & Practice*, *12*(1), 36–47.

Young, M. L., Kuo, F. Y., & Myers, M. D. (2012). To share or not to share: A critical research perspective on knowledge management systems. *European Journal of Information Systems*, *21*(5), 496–511.

Yu, M. (2014). Examining the effect of individualism and collectivism on knowledge sharing intention: An examination of tacit knowledge as moderator. *Chinese Management Studies*, *8*(1), 149–166.

Zhang, X. A., Cao, Q., & Grigoriou, N. (2011). Consciousness of social face: The development and validation of a scale measuring desire to gain face versus fear of losing face. *Journal of Social Psychology*, *151*(2), 129–149.

Zhao, Z., & Anand, J. (2009). A multilevel perspective on knowledge transfer: Evidence from the Chinese automotive industry. *Strategic Management Journal*, *30*(9), 959–983.

4 Comparative Case Studies

Early research identified learning-related barriers faced by developed multinational corporations (MNCs). Recent studies indicate how the diverse and idiosyncratic economic, social and institutional factors in Asia can induce an organization to blend global perspectives with local insights under the general assumption that knowledge management processes are socially constructed and are embedded in specific social contexts. The basic research question for this contextualist perspective focuses on how differences in cultural and institutional conditions among countries, such as home and host, influence the learning and knowledge management activities in MNCs? In order to answer the above research question, we conducted in-depth interviews with senior managers and frontline employees who worked in production plants in Brazil and China in order to have a better understanding of the cultural differences of knowledge sharing among workers in both countries based on content analysis of the responses (see Appendix I).

Case Study: GE Hydro

GE Hydro is an American MNC, and the two plants in Brazil and China, GE Hydro Brazil, and GE Hydro China, apply similar process and product lines in both countries to produce synchronous electrical generators (capital goods) for hydro-electrical power stations.

Inaugurated in 1958, GE Hydro Brazil was located in Sao Paulo. It currently has 700 direct employees. Among them, 80 are workers in the electrical lines, 170 are in the mechanical lines and 450 are employees in the administrative departments, including technicians, engineers and administrative personnel. This plant focuses on all Latin American countries and exports equipment and components for other Hydro GE's in North America and Europe for the hydro-electrical power stations of public and private constructing equipment companies.

Located in Tianjin, GE Hydro China plant was inaugurated in 1995. This plant has strong support from the Brazilian subsidiary during its launch. It currently has 1200 direct employees. Among them, 115 workers are in the electrical lines, 471 are in the mechanical lines and 620 are in the administrative structure technicians, engineers and administrative personnel. Targeting hydro-electrical power plants of public and private constructing equipment companies, this plant

DOI: 10.4324/9781003112136-4

focuses on all Asian countries and exports equipment and components to other Hydro GE's in North America and Europe.

The main products are hydraulic turbines and synchronous electrical generators, and both companies have an administrative structure comprising the Sales, Commercial, Engineering, Supply Chain, Finance, Industrial Engineering, Quality, IT, Project Management, Commissioning and Construction, Human Resources, Environmental Health and Safety Departments. Both plants have the same functional structure on the shop floor in which the production manager is supported by supervisor and production leaders. The production leaders deal directly with the workers, who are categorized based on their experience, and their promotions are related to the personal performance assessed by the production leaders.

The synchronous electrical generators are customized for each project to ensure enhanced performance for the unique hydro-electrical power stations conditions and customer needs. The production system is based on made-to-order projects for hydroelectric power stations, which allows consumers to purchase products that are customized according to their specifications. Synchronous electrical generators are produced to run smoothly under any operating condition, while reducing structural stress and improving reliability for the lifetime of the turbine. Figure 4.1 shows the 3D Image for a hydraulic Vertical Kaplan turbine for the synchronous electrical generator (Costilhas, 2020).

Figure 4.1 Vertical Kaplan turbine and synchronous electrical generator unit

Source: Image Credit – GE Renewable Energy (https://www.ge.com/renewableenergy/about-us/downloads).

The synchronous electrical generators have three independent manufacturing lines. In both countries, the production processes follow the value stream mapping and apply the lean and continuous improvement concepts (Alcântara, 2021). The processes are thus embedded into workers' tacit knowledge. The generator components produced in manufacturing lines are Stator Bar, Rotor Poles and Stator Lamination:

1 Stator winding bars/coils consist of assembling copper strands and insulation materials onto pieces that will conduct the magnetic flow coming from the rotor and transform it into power output. The manufacturing line starts with copper elementary strand, and it follows with the insulation material, mainly mica paper and epoxy resin, to form the insulation system. The finished stator bar should be electrically tested and dimensionally guaranteed to comply with the stator requirements. After that, it can be delivered piece by piece. This manufacturing line is supported by hydraulic press, taping machines, impregnation chambers and several hand tools.
2 Rotor poles: Pieces attached to the rotor structure that hold the copper windings where the excitation current will flow and then produce the magnetic field that will feed the stator core and windings. The production line starts with a copper straight bar, and carbon steel lamination. Some insulation materials, such as Nomex paper and epoxy resin, are also used to electrically insulate the components. After the rotor pole is assembled, it goes through a dimensional and electrical check. Single finished poles must be packed and delivered piece by piece. This manufacturing line is supported by laser cutting machines, press and brazing machines and other hand tools.
3 Stator core laminations: Pieces that fill and form the stator circumference when stacked are intended to absorb the magnetic field produced by the rotor poles and direct them to the stator winding where the power output will be generated. The definition for the stator core lamination production is simply an automated line considering a big press, which punches the lamination mostly made of silicon steel. Then it goes to a conveyor automatically and suffers deburring and insulation varnishing applied by a rubber roll. After curing, then in the end of the line, each lamination is stacked above the other, forming a single package of stator core lamination, then it will be delivered piece by piece. This manufacturing line is supported by punching machines, varnishing machines, spot welding machines and stacking robots.

The electrical and mechanical components produced in the electrical plant will go to the final assembly and testing, and due to their size, some generators are assembled directly on the hydro-electrical power stations.

Authority

Chinese workers strongly respect the hierarchical structure to make decisions in the work environment. Traditionally speaking, they appreciate a congruence between the organization's values and their own (Li & Ngo, 2017), and it ensures that Chinese manager's guidelines are implemented as an order by their employees.

> Chinese culture is strong, very traditional and with a lot of discipline and hierarchy. You must respect it.
>
> (MANCOMEN1)

> The level of positions is very clear in Chinese and Asian companies, and you can only report your work to your direct boss...
>
> (MANCOMEL2)

> Chinese culture has this motto … 'follow the boss.' If the boss tells you to do something wrong, you will do something wrong without any questions.
>
> (MANENGELE)

> Regarding the Chinese culture, I think that the Chinese work harder. They do not observe working hours, they always work overtime and they have a characteristic that they always find it easy to obey the boss' orders and they are also conservative …
>
> (MANCOMEL1)

> From top to bottom, it has the same structure, but the reaction from the bottom in China is different. The Chinese has the culture of not saying no and he/she will continue to work in the same way. That is already culture.
>
> (MANENGEL)

Brazilian workers are more flexible about following orders from hierarchical structure (Tong & Mitra, 2009). Brazilian workers also respect orders and informal agreements as well. They appreciate open dialogues to clarify the meanings about the order and/or guidelines.

> Here in Brazil, there is a greater freedom and questioning, "Have you thought about it?" "Couldn't this action cause a problem?" so, the Brazilian worker cultivate a more open dialog that differs from Chinese workers.
>
> (MANENGEL)

Salary is an issue that influences the power of authority in both countries, but in the Chinese context, it is stronger.

> I was a supervisor at the steel factory in China in 2014. It was easy to manage workers if you pay well. If you give more bonuses, more incentives, workers will work hard. It is easy to control the Chinese workers since the market is more competitive. If you want a job, you have to work harder. If you pay right, it is easy to deal with workers.
>
> (MANCOMELE1)

Guanxi

Guanxi refers to either the state of two or more parties being connected or the connected parties themselves. *Guanxi* in the Chinese work environment contributes to the enforceability of reciprocity, which is important for the development of a subordinate's trust in his or her supervisor (Wong, 2017). Under such a relational context at work, two people either have or do not have *guanxi* (Chen et al., 2018).

Managers and workers in both countries consider good relations at work as beneficial to their career development and good working climate. Chinese workers have *guanxi* most institutionalized among them, and it exists among Brazilians workers discreetly to avoid association with favouritism from a manager to a specific worker.

> Guanxi in China is stronger than in Brazil. If you want a career promotion, you need to maintain a good Guanxi relationship with supervisor with important people, because it creates strong dependence on the relationship. Asian countries are more dependent on this kind of relationship than other countries in the world. This indicates that bosses can determine more things…
>
> (MANCOMEL1)

The Chinese employee's performance is only evaluated by his/her superior, who does not necessarily share it with the employee.

> In China, when your boss does not like your job, he will not say anything. The bosses will give a note to each person and you do not know, only the bosses know. No one will explain why you will not have any bonuses or about no evolution in our career. This is what we call 'The Chiefs' right.'
>
> (MANCOMEL2)

Job Security

Job security is considered an antecedent of affective commitment, and the *guanxi* between subordinate and manager is also viewed as an antecedent of loyalty to manager (Wong, 2017). In some interviews, managers indicated that the knowledge sharing does not affect job security and someone indicated that it is not a sensitive matter in China due to its economic growth.

> Brazilians are more afraid of losing their job and because of this they strive a little more to focus on getting the results
>
> (MANENGEL)

> Chinese factories are more punitive towards workers because it is easy to look for a replacement for the worker. If you dismiss, it is easier to recruit a new one. There are more people to hire.
>
> (MANCOMEL1)

> In Brazil, employees seek more knowledge. Brazilians even pursue specializations and master's degrees, while in China you will not see many employees with master's degrees, because once the Chinese are employed, he ends up accommodating himself. [Employee focuses on the company and work]
>
> (MANENGEL)

On the other hand, Brazilian workers are afraid of losing jobs due to the unstable economic situation, but they are not afraid of losing their jobs for sharing knowledge with colleagues they trust.

> ... In Brazil, the relationship between workers is very friendly. Their knowledge is limited, but they used to share information/knowledge. They were not afraid of losing their jobs.
>
> (MANENGEL)

Brazilian workers consider relationships and personal ties when making their decisions. The Brazilian sociocultural roots support the paradigmatic Brazilian way (*jeitinho brasileiro*), which means a special way of managing obstacles influenced by interpersonal relationships in order to avoid the bureaucracy (Amado & Brasil, 1991).

The concern of employment for the government and unions has common roots in China. In Brazil, the triadic relationship among union-government-company has been separated and unions have recently lost their space due to new legislations with the withdrawal of labour rights and the elimination of the transfer of tax resources from employees/companies to support the unions (Passos & Lupatini, 2020).

> The Chinese come from a communist policy, where companies are more preventive. The chance of becoming unemployed is lower, and today there are many companies that do not belong to the government.
>
> (MANENGEL)

Face

Face is related to trust building in the social interactions between persons when at least one of whom is Chinese (King & Wei, 2018). The Chinese workers avoid exposing themselves and overlapping with his immediate superior. In Brazil, workers are encouraged to contribute to solving problems and expose themselves in the work context.

> Chinese workers cannot be transparent, so they don't appear smarter than the boss
>
> (MANCOMEN1)

Sometimes, the face behaviour indicates that some people are afraid to share their problems in the Chinese context.

> If something is not right, Chinese workers cannot be transparent… when there is a problem, he/she hide it…
>
> (MANCOMEN1)

Transparency

Transparency is related to the flows of open communication among individuals (Mc Manus et al., 2016). The Brazilian workers appreciate transparent behaviours as they encourage open dialogues and ask specific questions to clarify work-related issues. However, the face factor influences this transparent behaviour in a more discreet way in China.

> Chinese workers cannot be transparent, if something is not right it cannot be transparent, you must hide it when you have a problem, so you do not appear smarter than the boss. Chinese culture is strong, very traditional and with a lot of discipline and hierarchy, you must respect it.
>
> (MANCOMEN1)

Performance Orientation vs. Humane Orientation

Performance orientation refers to the degree in which a collective encourages and provides appropriate rewards to group members for their work performance (House et al., 2004). The Chinese economy provides employment opportunities for the Chinese workers and this is not a barrier to knowledge sharing. However, the Chinese GE plant is new and major part of employees are consolidating the technical knowledge.

> What happens is that China has been experiencing economic growth for a long time, so China is in a position to have employability, which makes the company to be the showcase of the employee and can change it at any time.
>
> (MANENGEL)

Some conflicts are created in both countries when we look for these aspects. Specifically, the Chinese company and their workers are closer of the union than their counterpart in Brazil.

> The Chinese union is strong with its well-structured office controlled by the government. The guy in the union checks out every week. In Brazil, when the employee does something stupid, he ends up being fired. There [China] you don't see much of it; the Chinese ends up changing the employee and trying to get it right.
>
> (MANENGEL)

Humane orientation refers to the degree to which a collective values individual for being fair, generous and caring about each other (House et al., 2004). The Brazilian plant has a longer history, and its workers have more experience about the processes. The Chinese plant is the newest and the worker follows the procedure as the main guide of production tasks in a more disciplined way.

> We Brazilians are not very formal in terms of writing paper and procedure. We place a lot of value on person-person contact. I think this last one [person-person contact] is a similarity between Brazil and China. That is why both the China manager and the Brazil manager valued this contact of speaking to transmit knowledge. I think this is a characteristic of Brazil and China managers.
>
> (MANENGEL)

> I think the Brazilian knows how to do it. I think he has little patience to keep elaborating a lot. You know, he already wants to go to the finals, and he already wants to go to action.
>
> (MANENGEL)

> As the plant is new and there is a high turnover, every time people change there. I think the Chinese employees have less knowledge than the Brazilians and less practical knowledge in the plant.
>
> (MANENGEL)

There is distinct behaviour related to social recognition between Brazil and China. The Brazilian workers appreciate public recognitions and the Chinese blue-collars employees receive basic wages. Moreover, the Chinese workers are also motivated by financial rewards.

> Brazilian likes recognition ..., and appreciate a recognition given from the boss and awarded in public, while the Chinese wants a financial incentive. He [Brazilian] wants people around to see the boss happy with his work.
>
> (MANENGEL)

> When the head of the area sees that an employee worked well, he usually gives a financial incentive at the end of the month that generates incredible benefits to obtain his engagement. Employees sometimes work so hard that they even not respect the Environment Health and Safety issues, but they meet the deadlines. While the Brazilian works within certain limits, it imposes a little more pressure to make an extra effort, while in China these limits are a little more flexible, so it has this advantage for China, because it manages to accelerate more.
>
> (MANENGEL)

Case Study: Maxion Wheels

This case is a Brazilian MNC which produces steel and aluminium wheels for cars, buses and trucks. Maxion Wheels is among the first automotive (Tier One) to implement a holistic innovation strategy that feeds and propels its advanced engineering work – a strategy with the aim of changing the future of mobility. The company has 3 engineering centres and 24 production plants in 15 countries, including South America, North America, Europe and Asia. The plant in China produces steel wheels and has a second joint venture under construction for a new aluminium wheel plant. Currently, the automotive wheel is the leader in sales with a production of 55 million wheels a year (Maxion, 2021).

Located in Sao Paulo State, Maxion Wheels Brazilian plant was inaugurated in 2016. It currently has 204 direct employees, including 75 indirect employees and 48 technicians/engineers. Its main customers are FCA/Jeep, Honda, Volkswagen, Jaguar Land Rover, Toyota and Renault. It produces aluminium wheels for light vehicles and has Production, Maintenance, Engineering, Sales, Human Resources, Finance, Industrial, IT and Safety, Health and Sustainability departments. The production plant is managed by a site manager who is assisted by supervisors, production leaders and workers responsible for direct activities on the shop floor. There are other two Brazilian plants located in other cities of Sao Paulo State.

Located in Jiangsu Province, the Chinese subsidiary of Maxion Nantong Wheels CO. Ltd was opened in 2008. It currently has 180 employees and its main customers are Iveco, Volvo, Michelin and Navistar. Maxion Wheels has a cross-cultural team of more than 10,000 employees who strive to improve transportations by serving their partners with the most advanced and competitive wheels, setting the benchmarks for developing and producing lighter, more cost-efficient, highly styled and smarter wheels. The steel wheels are for trucks and buses and have an organizational structure that includes the General Director of the Plant, Sales Manager, Finance, Human Resources, Production, Health-Safety-Environment, Maintenance, Quality and Engineering, serving the Asian and European market. The workers are classified into machine operator 1, machine operator 2, based on their experience about the operational processes, and there are operators categorized as specialized welding. A line leader who was a former operator organizes the operators' work and answers to the supervisor, who is led by a manager. In China, the job categories are similar, and there is no supervisor.

The Chinese plant was a greenfield company and the employees were hired with the lowest possible salary in the country. Some workers had experience in other companies, but it was the first job for others since most of them were farmers. In the beginning, it was not necessary for workers to have a basic level of education or technical course, and a great part of worker came from the countryside and went straight to work at the Maxion plant. This plant has strong support from the Brazilian subsidiary during its launch.

Authority

Chinese workers strongly respect hierarchy for decision-making in the work environment. In this work context, workers perceive a congruence between the norms and values of the organization and their own (Cleveland & Ellis, 2015). The Brazilian manager gives more explanation to support the meaning of his decisions and receives adherence to his/her instructions and tries to create a collaborative context. The Brazilian workers thus make more questions to understand the decision context and provide suggestions for improvements.

> The Brazilian manager has less authority and more commitment than the Chinese. In other words, the hierarchy is important and very strong in China. Sometimes, the boss is a military man. The hierarchy of the Chinese company is like an army and the Chinese bosses does not even talk to the shop floor workers. However, he treats all employees equally, and always respects the hierarchy. The Brazilian boss usually has a commitment and a strong relationship with everyone around him.
>
> (DIRAQAUT)

The automotive plant interviews also indicate authority in Chinese context as an important factor to influence work context, and the Chinese people respect formal leadership based on seniority and regardless of gender (male or female). The Brazilian workers engage in dialogues more with the managers in order to understand the reasons of the request and achieve good results.

> In China, hierarchy is strong, and the workers are very disciplined. They do not make a lot of questions, and they simply follow instructions. In Brazil, the workers make more question, until they understand why an instruction is important.
>
> (SUPAUT)

> The Chinese are influenced by Confucianism … some rules are hierarchy, respecting the elders, respecting the father of the family, a very strong patriarchal side, but in Asian cultures, China is where you find more women leaders. For this side of Confucianism, there are women with strategic and leadership positions in companies. They accept this hierarchy of having a woman in charge, no matter how much they have this respect within a patriarchal family structure headed by the father or the older brother. The mother stands out, but within the professional environment the woman can perform her leadership work.
>
> (DIRAQAUT)

Guanxi

Chinese managers and employees cultivate *guanxi* to facilitate achievements and career advancement, including informal events off-site to connect the employees.

> When the plant achieves outstanding production target, it is common for the supervisors and managers to have drinking and eating together to celebrate. This is traditional for them… The Chinese have some cultural traditions, like "Losing Face" and "Guanxi"… The Chinese managers tried to focus not only on the financial aspect but on the personal too, appreciating all employee´s efforts. The boss is (Lauban) always encouraging and recognizing subordinates' efforts. But the strongest point of the Chinese is the financial one.
>
> (DIRAQAUT)

Job Security

Low knowledge sharing (knowledge hiding) is sometimes associated with fear of losing job (Durst et al., 2019). The consistent growth of the Chinese economy creates job security and employment opportunities. Brazil is experiencing a different scenario, with the plants stop producing automobiles in the country, such as Ford (Oxford Analytica, 2021), and reduction in labour force. In this regard, managers recognize the importance of worker knowledge sharing on the shop floor.

> What happens is that China has been experiencing economic growth for a long time, so China is in a position to achieve full employment, which makes the company as the showcase of the employee, who can change him/her at any time.
>
> (DIROPAUT)

> The relationship between the Chinese co-workers was very friendly. Their knowledge was limited, and they are used to share the information and not afraid of losing their jobs.
>
> (SUPAUT)

> The Chinese worker is proactive, likes to learn, has no day-and-time limitation and considers his job as his own business. The problem is that the Chinese do not like to share knowledge with each other for fear of losing their job, so it is difficult to work as a team with them.
>
> (DIRAUTO)

> Here in Brazil, the operators' concern about sharing knowledge or developing a colleague for fear of losing their job is more visible. It has gone down a lot over the years, but it still exists.
>
> (ENGAUTO)

Face

Face is relevant in Chinese business practice and can be traded, or at least considered, in negotiations. Recognition based on knowledge is a relevant incentive to Brazilian.

> Brazilians like to have recognition. They do not need a promotion [relatively speaking], but a recognition from the boss, while the Chinese wants financial incentive and recognition in public. They want people around to see the boss happy with his/her work...like to improve guanxi ...gain Face.
>
> (DIROPAUT)

> You have to be very careful in China in pointing out failures and mistakes to the employee in front of others, what the Chinese calls losing face. This is extremely important, if you make one of your subordinates lose face in front of others ... you will lose that person. You will no longer be able to work with him/her. They will no longer perform activities, and you will have to find a position in another place for him/her. This is very serious in their culture.
>
> (DIRAQAUT)

Transparency

Brazilian managers avoid reprimanding employees in public and need to explain his/her concerns about the employee in details.

> In Brazil, they talk to indicate their concerns about employees' tasks [reprimand] privately and explain in a transparent way.
>
> (DIROPAUT)

Performance Orientation vs. Humane Orientation

As for the humane orientation dimension, both countries care a lot about having favourable social conditions and rewards in their work context.

> There is more camaraderie/companionship in China than here [Brazil] because people are more committed to each other (complementing each other). Here in Brazil, it is easier to find an employee complaining when another one is doing something wrong and not in China. They are more complacent and help each other more.
>
> (DIROPAUT)

Besides, the Chinese workers value the interests and respect for their culture.

> When there is a foreigner that respects their Chinese culture and tries to understand them, they make everything easier. It is important to respect their culture and show the necessary results, so that you can have success together.
>
> (SUPAUT)

The differences in social and macroeconomic contexts between Brazil and China, and the union's influence, affect both countries' orientation towards performance. Some conflicts are generated in both countries when we look at these aspects, including the Chinese company and workers are closer to the union than in Brazil.

> The Chinese union is strong, with its well-structured office being led the government. The guy in the union checks out every week.
>
> (SUPAUT)

> The Government controls everything in China. There was a labor union in every company. In our factory, we had one in the planning area. They work very well, but they share all the information to the union. The government is the union. In China, they have a′leasing regime′, and the factory was not ours. Every time the government could take it. It was a 60-70 years contract.
>
> (DIRAQAUT)

In a broader context, traditionalism and collectivism are keys to sharing knowledge in the industrial environment. Respecting culture is essential in both countries.

> When a foreigner respects the Chinese culture and tries to understand it, things get much easier. It is important to respect the culture and show the need to obtain results....
>
> (SUPAUT)

> Here in Brazil, operators' concern about not sharing knowledge or developing a colleague for fear of losing their jobs is more visible. It has decreased a lot over the years, but it still exists.
>
> (SUPAUT)

> The Chinese saw Brazilians working as a team, but it is not a natural characteristic of the Chinese. For example, if a part was missing for the Chinese operator to work, he would sit down to rest.
>
> (SUPAUT)

The Chinese prefer to share knowledge based on technical documentation (internalization), respecting the hierarchy in a disciplined way, while Brazilians enjoy working in groups and have no difficulty in transmitting tacit knowledge to other colleagues in the organization through socialization.

Both workers are motivated by financial incentives, but the Chinese workers have this most salient characteristic. They have no personalized commitment to the organization and changed jobs due to any increase in salary for many reasons, including the all-too-common reason for supporting their parents when they are the only child in the family. The Brazilian worker, on the other hand, has a greater commitment to the organization in which he/she works and is also motivated by the recognition of his/her managers.

For the fear of losing his job, the Chinese worker does not share knowledge with colleagues, especially foreigners. On the other hand, Brazilians are less disciplined but work well in teams.

> The Chinese are motivated when their performance is recognized through better wages ... they did not care about the number of hours that it was necessary to work to have this financial part rewarded
>
> (SUPAUTO)

> Brazilians like to have recognition, not necessarily they want a promotion, but recognition from the manager, while the Chinese worker wants financial rewards and public recognition. He wants people to be around to see how happy his boss is with his job. They do not like to lose face
>
> (DIROPAUT)

Case Study: Toyota

Toyota Motor Corporation was founded in 1937 and has 359,542 employees operating in over 160 countries nowadays, including 3 head offices in Japan and 65 production plants around the world. Among them, 50 production plants are located outside Japan (Toyota, 2021), which include those in Brazil and China.

In 1958, the first Toyota plant outside Japan was inaugurated in Brazil. Toyota Brazil started the Complete Knock-Down (CKD) production of the Land Cruiser Bandeirante vehicle in 1961. CKD, as a modality, is a collection of parts from other regions (i.e., Japan) to be assembled in the region (i.e., Brazil). In 1962, it started to manufacture the Brazilian Bandeirante model, which was a reference in the Brazilian utility market for 40 years in Sao Bernardo do Campo, Sao Paulo state.

In 2012, the third factory was opened in Sorocaba (SP), which is currently responsible for the production of the Etios, Yaris and Corolla Cross models which are exported to 22 countries. This unit has a production capacity of 120,000 vehicles/year. In 2016, Toyota opened the engine production plant in the city of Porto Feliz (SP), responsible for producing 200,000 engines/year. In 2023, the Toyota plant located in Sao Bernardo do Campo will be closed. Toyota Brazil currently has four distribution centres in Brazil and four manufacturing units with an installed capacity of 170,000 vehicles/year. In total, it has 5,700 employees involved in the production of the Etios, Yaris and Corolla Cross models.

Toyota China was established in 2004 as a joint venture between Japanese automaker Toyota Motor Company and GAC Toyota Motor Co Ltd (GTMC). The GTMC is the main plant in China, and it is located in Shinan Da Dao City, Nansha District, Guangzhou, Guangdong, China. In 2006, the company began producing Toyota brand vehicles, such as Camry, Yaris Highlander, Camry Hybrid, E'Z, Levi-Corolla and C-HR, for China and exporting to other Asian countries. Currently, its two production lines have a combined capacity of 500,000 vehicles/year with 7,000 employees.

The work arrangements of Toyota are the same in Brazil and China. There are three categories of workers (Operator 1, 2 and 3), and the progression is for every 2 years based on the skill acquisitions via formal training. They report to a team leader who leads a team of 8–12 operators. There is a group leader to manage three to four team leaders, who in turn reports to a supervisor. Then a manager manages three to four supervisors. The promotions for team leaders and group leaders are based on the employee's own initiative according to the availability of vacancies, practical and theoretical evaluation of their knowledge and skills. Supervision and management promotions are aligned with the company's strategy and the employee's performance records, which are the main criteria for nominating the employee to the vacancy.

Authority

The distance of communication between workers and managers is longer in China than in Brazil due to the respect for authority. In Toyota Brazil, the communications between managers and workers are more open with a focus to contribute to task improvements and knowledge sharing, while the Chinese managers are more autocratic.

> In Brazil, the relation among people is more friendly between supervisors and the team members. In China, it is like an army, which means that the supervisor is very, very strong... There are a long distance of communication between the supervisor and workers... he [supervisor or manager] stays in a very high position... the team members and the team leaders respect the supervisors a lot. So, they [team members and the team leaders] must follow 100% of the supervisors... but in Brazil, I can see a more friendly relationship, and the supervisor also can manage the team members efficiently. There is good communication between a supervisors and members and the work can be done... Brazilian team members can say their opinion.
>
> (MANPRODTOY)

> In China, there is no negotiation. The supervisor or manager simply called team meeting to give the guidelines, objectives, tasks of the day and the execution just follows, ...in Brazil it is different. It is based on negotiation... it depends on the work environment [relationship], if it is good, you can simply call the leaders and the team to pass the actions and they execute... if the environment is not good within the team, you have to explain the assignment in more details, give incentive and indicate gains for them and for the company...
>
> (MANPRODTOY)

> ... as they [Chinese] have a high level of commitment and respect for the hierarchy. If the boss tells him/her to do something, he will stay straight... working for 50 hours direct if is necessary to deliver what was asked.
>
> (MANENGTOY)

A lack of open communication between managers and workers sometimes brings problems related to the "blinded" execution just based on manager orientation, because reduced autonomy creates risks involved in the decision requested.

> The point I emphasize is about this commitment [Chinese].... but in some cases, it can be a disadvantage... They do not question much and as they respect a lot of hierarchy, if the boss says do it, they end up not thinking and follow automatically... so if you have a good and strong manager, the whole team ends up giving great results ...
>
> (MANENGTOY)

Guanxi

Guanxi orientation is defined as interpersonal relationship in which individuals consider themselves and others for the purpose of fixing their own role and reacting to strangers and is an important component of social orientation in China (Su et al., 2003). Chinese workers indicate that there is a positive influence between *guanxi* and knowledge sharing. Brazilian culture is influenced by interpersonal relationship and the feelings of kindness and concern for other individuals. Interpersonal relationships are important for professional career development. People search, relate harmoniously, and contribute to a good relationship with colleagues and managers for supporting knowledge sharing.

> It has the goal in Brazil, but if there is no trust, there is a difficulty in engaging others.
>
> (MANPRODTOY)

Reciprocal relationships influence social interactions related to knowledge sharing (Ding et al., 2017). The Brazilian and Chinese indicate that knowledge sharing strengths the relationships with other colleagues and contribute to integration with other members of the organization and relationship between members sharing a common interest. The Brazilian workers consider affection and interpersonal relationships in their decisions to solve working tasks, and the Chinese workers are very focused on achieving the goals and outcomes requested by the superior and managers. Since an objective is determined, all efforts are dedicated towards achieving it.

> Brazilians need more dialogues and explanations and are influenced by affection. In China, the goal is more relevant. Once determined, it is pursued. But if there is no trust, there is a difficulty in engaging the worker in Brazil...
>
> (MANPRODTOY)

> [workers] are very shy in China, but they are more direct to achieve the results and are disciplined about work method [TPS] than Brazilians. Brazilians are more sentimental. You [manager] need to persuade them to do a job or reach some goals... once you make the requests to the [Chinese] workers, they will pursue that goal regardless of the work environment and their emotional state.
>
> (MANPRODTOY)

> In China, the positive point is the results orientation, the level of concentration and meeting goals are very strong ... we have the relationship, the habit of coffee breaks for chats to share ideas [among employees] in Brazil. There is a very strong human orientation and attention to improve relationships... in China this does not exist... they start to work with a very well-defined routine and contribute to meeting their goals... Brazilians have the facility to exchange information. They have a more affectionate relationship among employees, which also contributes to achieve the objectives. In China, there is not... communication is less...the teamwork in Brazil is different...the Asian people are shy in the way of treating people...
>
> (MANPRODTOY)

Job Security

Toyota motor company has a tradition of maintaining employment at all of its facilities, even when productivity gains come from continuous improvement. In Brazil and China, layoffs occur in particular cases based on demands reduction, but there is usually a job-keeping effort at Toyota that stands out from other companies in the automotive industry.

> In Japan, job security is part of an agreement between the company and the union, and the other plants of the group follow this guideline. In Brazil, we try to keep the employment, but in some cases the employee is fired.
>
> (MANPRODTOY)

Face

Facing saving is understood as a behaviour to avoid negative evaluation and sustain social position in potentially harmful situations (Keil et al., 2007). Although face issues are common in eastern countries, the Brazilian workers show knowledge sharing behaviour underpinned by this cultural value. Brazilian workers indicate that there is a positive influence between knowledge sharing and face saving that affects other's perception. Knowledge sharing influences the importance given to how other colleagues see him/herself. Face gaining refers to a behaviour to maintain and promote people's positive image and social self-worth. People with a tendency to face gaining are more associated with positive perception and a tendency to reinforce their public image (Chou, 1997).

Brazilians tend to be more confident to share knowledge with their colleagues and like to share knowledge in public to have greater visibility in the work context. Brazilian employees seem to be willing to ask questions more often without much concern for being perceived boastful or immodest. Employees perceived knowledge sharing as enhancing their prospects of future job promotions (Muniz et al., 2019).

The Chinese workers indicate a different judgement as compared to the Brazilians when referring to facing saving. The Chinese gave less importance to how other colleagues see them, and about the inconvenience generated by non-fulfilment of their requests.

> When it is identified that an operation is causing a lot of defects, the worker is taken off the line for training [in Brazil]. This is often understood as a fault exposition at work in China.
>
> (MANPRODTOY)

Chinese respondents are indifferent to sharing their knowledge in public under requests and are more reluctant to share their knowledge in public. The public recognition is very important to the Brazilian workers, but not for Chinese workers.

> The worker likes recognition and exposes his kaizen in public in Brazil.
>
> (MANPRODTOY)

> An important motivational incentive for Brazilians is to have recognition, even with a simple thank you, when someone makes an improvement [kaizen], and you thank the employee for showing the manager's and the company's recognition of the employee's contribution, presentation is well received...in China, I do not see it that much... It [kaizen - improvements] is understood as an obligation. You have to keep on doing it. There is no thank you. Motivational recognition is important for making the workers proud in Brazil...
>
> (MANPRODTOY)

Transparency

In China, there is a cultural tradition in favour of collective gains and there is more trust about the company by workers. The managers need to pay a particular attention to discuss some sensitive issues with workers in Brazil, such as their annual bonus.

> I see a similar situation between the oldest plant in Brazil [Sao Bernardo do Campo] and Japan [Tahara] about discussions involving employees, either because the Asians are more peaceful, so the discussions are always very focused. You end up seeing interests are not just a form of individualism,

> only the operator or company side...and the whole process is more transparent... When the company won, how much the company is selling, how much bonus can be transferred... how much new investments it will have... so the discussion ends up being more relaxed.
>
> (MANENGTOY)

> The financial recognition in Brazil needs to be discussed further with the employees. He wants to know more details about how it is calculated. For example, he participates in the discussion of annual bonuses. In China, this is done by the company and soon it is not questioned by the workers. Here in Brazil the worker needs more details. There is a concern that the company and employee have won, not only the company...
>
> (MANPRODTOY)

> The Chinese employee communicates less. This occurs when there are meetings with the team and he has to make some presentation of some improvement. In Brazil without asking he [worker] naturally shares both the positive side and something negative about what happens on the line.
>
> (MANPRODTOY)

Performance Orientation vs. Humane Orientation

Toyota develops their employees internally, and the company prefers to hire people without previous experience. In this way, Toyota avoids bringing some practices from other companies that are against its culture, and the managers indicate that cultural influence in the work is observed throughout the plants under study.

> Both countries have positive sides but the cultures are different... Brazilian culture does influence the plant work...
>
> (MANPRODTOY)

> Toyota does not hire people with experience so as not to bring vices from other companies. It prefers young people and recent undergraduates... Brazilians have a characteristic that when they come from other companies, it is difficult to change their minds... difficult to introduce Toyota's principles, which is a different mindset from other companies ...
>
> (MANPRODTOY)

The knowledge sharing intention refers to the desire and willingness of individuals to share their knowledge with others (Reychav & Weisberg, 2010). Brazilian and Chinese respondents indicate that there is a positive influence between reciprocal relationship with their colleagues and knowledge sharing. The Brazilian and Chinese workers share knowledge with their colleagues. The Brazilians do that voluntarily, and Chinese will do more when they are requested.

> In Brazil, workers cultivate bonds with co-workers...In China, employees do not talk to each other much, and there is no event outside the company. In Brazil, the relationship is more cultivated through informal gatherings outside the factory (barbecue, soccer game) that also include the family...
>
> (MANPRODTOY)

Sense of self worth assesses the degree to which the employee believes his/her behaviour can contribute to the organization's functioning (Bock et al., 2005). People gain a strong sense of worth when they feel their knowledge is meaningful to the people around them in the organizations (Ding et al., 2017). There is a positive influence between knowledge sharing and sense of self-worth among Brazilian and Chinese workers in Toyota related to improvement of work processes in the organization, thus increasing productivity in the organization, helping other members to solve problem and achieving the organization's goals.

The role of the union is totally different in the two countries. In Brazil, the union is not seen as a partner by the company. In China, the union is a partner. The behaviour of union in Brazil is not unique. It differs based on maturity of the labour relation of the region where a plant is located.

> The union relationship with Toyota in Brazil varies according to the region where the plant is located, with some plants having a balanced relationship and others with a more conflicting and distrustful relationship...
>
> (MANENGTOY)

> In Brazil, the union member is not well regarded. He confronts the company. There is mistrust... In Asia, the profit is seen as an investment for the company's future.
>
> (MANPRODTOY)

The Brazilian union representative is an effective communication channel between the worker and the company, who raises the workers' issues and tries to solve them (i.e., wages).

> The worker in the daily routine does not find the opportunity for dialogues with his/her manager about personal claims. He finds this opportunity with the union... we managers have the difficulty in sustaining a closer relationship due to the work routine... there is specific needs of the worker...the unionist raises these opportunities [needs] on the assembly lines... today the union is an interlocutor for the employee. He listened to some sensitive needs...in Brazil the unionist is dedicated to union tasks and does not work in production... in China he works directly on the assembly line.
>
> (MANPRODTOY)

Reward refers to employee satisfaction due to an economic incentive for their knowledge sharing behaviour (Hau et al., 2013). It is noted among the Brazilian respondents that there is a positive influence between rewards and knowledge sharing (Muniz, Ribeiro, et al., 2021; Muniz, Wintersberger, et al., 2021). And there is a distinction among the Chinese respondents who judged that the sharing of knowledge does not influence the obtaining of financial reward and has no impact for promotion (Sacho, 2021). The procedures of promotions and salaries are different for the Brazilians. The growth of Chinese professionals is based on the time of working in the company and, consequently, the experience within the company, whereas professional growth occurs through individual achievement of goals in Brazil.

> There is not much meritocracy there. The important point is time with the company... The operator enters, and he knows his career plan, such as how long it will take in his position, where he will be in five years. It will evolve from being an operator to becoming a leader in 10 years, so they do not have that ambition that we see here in Brazilians, which is to grow faster. So, it ends up in disfavoring meritocracy a little in my point of view. For example, a bonus has very clear rules ... very transparent. If we sell so many cars, the bonus will be five times of the basic salary or 10 times, so people have a greater commitment not to stop the line, like I do not know if the engagement is natural due to commitment or due to financial incentive...... here in Brazil, for every suggestion that operators give, they earn 10-20$. So, you see operators taking papers [forms] home and then bringing them back to receive financial return. On the other hand, the bonus is not very clear. Every time when the base date arrives, there is a certain tension and discussion... The line stops.
>
> (MANENGTOY)

> The process of evolution of promotions in China is very slow... I will do it here in five years. I will earn my moment. I will move up a step in the career of operator 1- 2- 3 and in Brazil, he knows that if he stands out ... he can become a leader. So, it generates positive competition, and seeking not only financial rewards. It is not just this anticipated advance; he ends up also seeking recognition from the leadership.
>
> (MANPRODTOY)

Conclusion

Poleacovschi et al. (2018) identify some labour characteristics, such as hierarchy level, education, language and cultural differences, as factors that might explain worker's attitude and intention towards knowledge sharing. Generally speaking, the Chinese employees are more work-oriented, whereas the Brazilian workers focus more on the relationship in their decisions related to work. These are some differences that influence knowledge sharing in the industry context.

Our findings indicate that respects for authority and hierarchy have a strong influence in the Chinese context, and it creates a distance to open dialogue to support worker knowledge sharing. The Brazilian managers and workers are more intimate during the improvements tasks, and the decisions are thoroughly discussed to promote engagement. There is knowledge sharing among the Brazilian operators despite the economic instability that has affected employment. Moreover, the Brazilians are motivated by informal recognition and financial incentives, whereas the union and company have close relationships in Chinese companies. Besides, the Chinese workers are more motivated by financial incentive, which is more unusual than in the Brazilian companies.

The findings indicate that Brazilian and Chinese managers have a similar judgement regarding the influence of culture on the relationship in both countries. However, different behaviours are observed between Brazilian and Chinese workers for face saving and face gaining and financial rewards, which are influenced by cultural aspects.

References

Alcântara, M. B. S. A. (2021). Cultura e Gestão do Conhecimento: um estudo comparativo em fábricas de rodas no Brasil e na China [Portuguese]; Culture and Knowledge Management: a comparative study of wheel factories in Brazil and China [Master's thesis]. School of Engineering of Guaratingueta, Sao Paulo State University, UNESP Repository.

Amado, G., & Brasil, H. V. (1991). Organizational behaviours and cultural context: The Brazilian "jeitinho". *International Studies of Management & Organization*, *21*(3), 38–61.

Bock, G.-W., Zmud, R. W., Kim, Y.-G., & Lee, J.-N. (2005). Behavioral intention formation in knowledge sharing: Examining the roles of extrinsic motivators, social-psychological forces, and organizational climate. *MIS Quarterly*, *29*(1), 87–111.

Chen, M. H., Chang, Y. Y., & Lin, Y. C. (2018). Exploring creative entrepreneurs' happiness: cognitive style, guanxi and creativity. *International Entrepreneurship and Management Journal*, *14*(4), 1089–1110.

Chou, M.-L. (1997). *Protective and acquisitive face orientations*. University of Hong Kong Press.

Cleveland, S., & Ellis, T. J. (2015, January). The impact of role conflict, role ambiguity, and locus of control on organizational knowledge sharing practices. In *2015 48th Hawaii International Conference on System Sciences* (pp. 3801–3810). IEEE.

Costilhas, A. A. M. (2020). Workers knowledge sharing improvements and the cultural influence: Comparative study Brazil and China in a capital good industry [Master's thesis]. School of Engineering of Guaratingueta, Sao Paulo State University, Unesp Repository: https://repositorio.unesp.br/handle/11449/202394.

Ding, G., Liu, H., Huang, Q., & Gu, J. (2017). Moderating effects of guanxi and face on the relationship between psychological motivation and knowledge-sharing in China. *Journal of Knowledge Management*, *21*(5), 1077–1097.

Durst, S., Hinteregger, C., & Zieba, M. (2019). The linkage between knowledge risk management and organizational performance. *Journal of Business Research*, *105*, 1–10.

Hau, Y. S., Kim, B., Lee, H., & Kim, Y.-G. (2013). The effects of individual motivations and social capital on employees' tacit and explicit knowledge sharing intentions. *International Journal of Information Management*, *33*(2), 356–366.

Hong, J., Snell, R. S., & Rowley, C. (2017). Conclusion: Challenges for organizational learning—institutional contexts, cross-border knowledge and context. In *Organizational Learning in Asia* (pp. 187–192). Elsevier.

House, R. J., Hanges, P. J., Javidan, M., Dorfman, P. W., & Gupta, V. (Eds.). (2004). *Culture, leadership, and organizations: The GLOBE study of 62 societies.* Sage publications.

Keil, M., Im, G. P., & Mähring, M. (2007). Reporting bad news on software projects: The effects of culturally constituted views of face-saving. *Information Systems Journal, 17*(1), 59–87.

King, P. C., & Wei, Z. (2018). The role of face in a Chinese context of trust and trust building. *Cross Cultural Management, 18*(2), 149–173.

Li, H., & Ngo, H. Y. (2017). Chinese traditionality, job attitudes, and job performance: A study of Chinese employees. *Evidence-Based HRM, 5*(2), 139–150.

Maxion. (2021). Maxion Wheels [Web page]. https://www.maxionwheels.com/company

Mc Manus, P., Ragab, M., Arisha, A., & Mulhall, S. (2016, September). Review of factors influencing employees' willingness to share knowledge. In *Proceedings of the 18th European Conference on Knowledge Management (ECKM).*

Muniz, J., Jr., Hong, J., Oliveira, S., Wintersberger, D., & Popadiuk, S. (2019). Knowledge sharing in the automotive sector: A comparative study of Chinese and Brazilian firms. *Production, 29*(1), 1–21.

Muniz, J. Jr, Ribeiro, V. B., & Pradhan, N. (2021). Knowledge-based assessment applied to lean Brazilian Toyota plants: Employees' perceptions. *International Journal of Knowledge Management, 17*(2), 1–22.

Muniz, J., Jr., Wintersberger, D., & Hong, J. L. (2021). Worker and manager judgments about factors that facilitate knowledge-sharing: Insights from a Brazilian automotive assembly line. *Knowledge and Process Management* (early view). doi: 10.1002/kpm.1693.

Oxford Analytica. (2021). Ford factory closures raise recovery fears in Brazil. *Emerald Expert Briefings,* (oxan-es). https://doi.org/10.1108/OXAN-ES258715

Passos, S. D. S., & Lupatini, M. (2020). A contrarreforma trabalhista e a precarização das relações de trabalho no Brasil (Portuguese). *Revista Katálysis, 23,* 132–142.

Poleacovschi, C., Javernick-Will, A., Tong, T., & Wanberg, J. (2018). Engineers seeking knowledge: Effect of control systems on accessibility of tacit and codified knowledge. *Journal of Construction Engineering and Management, 145*(2), 04018128.

Reychav, I., & Weisberg, J. (2010). Bridging intention and behavior of knowledge sharing. *Journal of Knowledge Management, 14*(2), 285–300.

Sacho, A. J. (2021). Cultura organizacional e sua influência no compartilhamento de conhecimento: o caso Toyota Brasil e China. [[Portuguese]; Organizational Culture and its Influence on Knowledge Sharing: the Toyota Brazil and China Case [Master's thesis]. School of Engineering of Guaratingueta, Sao Paulo State University, Unesp Repository: https://repositorio.unesp.br/bitstream/handle/11449/216851/sacho_aj_me_guara.pdf?sequence=3

Su, C., Sirgy, M. J., & Littlefield, J. E. (2003). Is guanxi orientation bad, ethically speaking? A study of Chinese enterprises. *Journal of Business Ethics, 44*(4), 303–312.

Tong, J., & Mitra, A. (2009). Chinese cultural influences on knowledge management practice. *Journal of Knowledge Management, 13*(2), 49–62.

Toyota. (2021). Toyota World [Web page]. http://www.global.toyota.com/

Wong, Y.-T. (2017). Affective commitment, loyalty to supervisor and guanxi: Chinese Employees in joint ventures and reformed state-owned enterprises. *Journal of Chinese Human Resource Management, 8*(2), 77–93.

5 Cross-cultural Analysis of Knowledge Sharing in China and Brazil

As discussed in previous chapters, Chinese and Brazilian cultures affect workers' knowledge sharing on the shop floor. In particular, production workers in these two countries demonstrate vastly different approaches on knowledge sharing. On one hand, Brazilian workers are more enthusiastic about knowledge sharing with other co-workers (Ardichvili et al., 2012; Muniz, Wintersberger, et al., 2021), while preferring to share knowledge through conversations among co-workers (socialization). On the other hand, Chinese workers prefer the internalization of written procedures, and they strongly respect hierarchy by avoiding to openly express opinions that are divergent from those of the superiors (Muniz et al., 2019).

In this regard, further research about how culture influences knowledge management (Ardichvili et al., 2006; Goswami et al., 2021; Hong et al., 2006; Muniz et al., 2019) is necessary. Drawing from a particularistic approach, the main research questions for this chapter focus on identifying what ways and to what extent workers' and managers' perspectives about knowledge sharing on the shop floor differ and the corresponding culture-specific factors that can enable knowledge sharing?

Context of Study

We have chosen production assembly lines as the empirical context of our study due to their complex and knowledge-intensive nature. Manual assembly process demands a lot of context-specific tacit knowledge and covers all areas of production activities through human and/or machine interaction. Assembly lines require a large number of decisions being delegated to the operators (skilled and non-skilled). The assembly line work has revealed the re-valuation of worker skills (Hu et al., 2011; Muniz, Wintersberger, et al., 2021) as below:

- Increasing product variety on an assembly line requires greater knowledge and skills from workers to respond to different assembly procedures (Hu et al., 2011);
- Decisions related to handling equipment, tightening torque and developing a sense of assembly are based on knowledge, memory, experience and skills, which are not always available in instructions and formal training (Kotha, 1995).

DOI: 10.4324/9781003112136-5

In the study, we investigated two manufacturing plants located in Brazil and China equipped with semi-automatic assembly lines and similar process in which tacit knowledge of the workers was applied in daily routines and continuous improvements were engaged by the workers, production leaders and plant managers (see description details in Chapter 4).

- Maxion Wheels, a Brazilian MNC, has production plants around the world with car wheels as its main product. We selected the Brazilian plant (80 years old) and the Chinese plant (15 years old) that produce the same products in assembly lines (Alcântara, 2021);
- GE Hydro, an American MNC, has production plants in Brazil and China that produce synchronous electrical generators (capital goods) for hydropower stations (Costilhas, 2020).

AHP Methodology

The problem of selecting workers' knowledge sharing factors, establishing a relationship among them and assessing their influence on the shop floor context is a case of multiple-criteria decision-making (MCDM). MCDM occurs in situations where more than one criterion is considered and these criteria (i.e., knowledge sharing factors) have a different judgment of importance for people involved in the same decision context (i.e., managers, production leaders, workers). Usually, different judgments' perspectives induce conflicts, which are minimized by using MCDM. The analytic hierarchy process (AHP) is a MCDM technique, which application is effective for ranking alternatives (Muniz et al., 2019). In this study, we chose to use AHP to identify different factors that affect worker knowledge sharing in the industrial environment based on the perception of each interviewee (workers and managers). In this way, the potential conflicts in judgment can be minimized by the use of multi-criteria methods.

The Incomplete Pairwise Comparison (IPC-AHP) is a MCDM technique by reducing the number of comparisons and completion time per respondent in order to ensure more reliable and more complete responses based on higher attention of the respondents to answer, and it is effective for ranking of factors (see e.g., Muniz et al., 2019; Muniz, Wintersberger, et al., 2021).

Analytic Hierarchy Process

Traditionally, production management models are composed of two dimensions: the technical dimension and the social dimension. Muniz et al. (2010a, 2010b) indicate that knowledge sharing among blue-collar workers is socially constructed in a model of knowledge management on the shop floor based on the integration of the following three dimensions (see details in Chapter 2):

- Knowledge: A set of systematic, formal and deliberate actions aimed at capturing, preserving, sharing and reusing tacit and explicit knowledge created

and used by people during routine improvement and production processes, thus generating measurable results for the organization and individuals;
- People: All issues related to job design as well as other HRM practices;
- Process: The management of tangible resources used in the production process of services and goods.

The use of IPC-AHP (Harker, 1987) as a multi-criteria decision technique decomposes complex decision-making problems (i.e., with multiple judgments at different levels) into sub-problems with hierarchical levels. Each hierarchical level represents a set of attributes or alternatives related to each sub-problem. The top level of the entire hierarchy represents the goal of the problem, which in the presented study, as effective knowledge sharing among blue-collar workers. An important step for the IPC-AHP method is the structuring of the decision problem into hierarchical levels and the construction of a model that relates the factors in terms of their priorities. In this step, the overall objective, the criteria and the alternatives are identified. Next, the judgments issued by people involved with the decision in question are collected. Following the identification of the objective (effective sharing of worker knowledge), we discerned three major sub-categories, namely socialization (dialogue), externalization (written down codes of practice and rules) as well as internalization (the studying and/or reading of such codes of practices and rules) at the next level. Finally, we considered different alternative tools to reach the means of better knowledge sharing, some of which included alternatives, including formal communication channels, forging of informal personal relationships (see details in Chapter 2).

Under each of these three broad dimensions, there are different enabling factors to provide support and incentives among blue-collar workers in a production environment (Erden et al., 2008; Nakano et al., 2013). The factors identified in the literature that indicate the integration of People, Knowledge and Process dimensions and support knowledge conversion as shown in the IPC-AHP structure (Figure 5.1).

Process factors contribute to the control and improvement of the daily activities of workers. These include problem-solving methods and standard operating procedure (SOP), all of which have been demonstrably found to promote workers to use and share their knowledge alongside increasing their levels of engagement (Muniz et al., 2010a, 2010b; Muniz, Ribeiro, et al., 2021).

The large number of factors (12) indicated above would have required a large number of pairwise comparisons (132) which would have most likely led to respondent fatigue during the survey completion. Therefore, the IPC-AHP (Harker, 1987) application reduces the number of comparisons and completion time to about 20 minutes per respondent in order to ensure more reliable and more complete responses.

Data Collection

The opinions from assembly workers, production leaders and managers from both the Brazilian and Chinese plants (Table 5.1) were collected. The workers

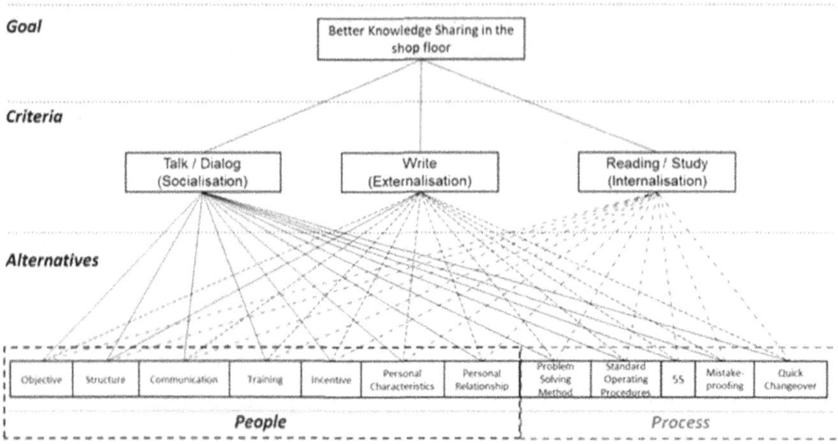

Figure 5.1 Hierarchical factors supporting knowledge sharing among production workers

Source: Muniz, Wintersberger, et al. (2021).

are young employees who begin their training on the lines and are assisted by the most experienced workers. The most experienced ones often did not have formal study but have acquired training on the job. Both companies train workers on its production lines, because electric synchronous generators and wheels production are very specific and tacit knowledge is relevant in these processes.

A pairwise comparison was then conducted to indicate the relative order of importance between different factors that affect knowledge sharing on the shop floor context based on their judgement and experience by using five-point Likert type (Saaty, 1988) as exemplified in Figure 5.2. The questionnaire (Appendix II) was developed and translated by both authors who are native speakers in Brazilian (Portuguese) and Chinese (Mandarin) language.

Table 5.2 provides an example of data analysis for three factors of one respondent. The comparison of the factors in each matrix was made between the horizontal and vertical elements in the matrix. Regarding the criteria (Table 5.2), the analysis and choice of the respondent allow us to conclude that conversation

Table 5.1 IPC-AHP respondents by plants

Plants		*Position*			
		Managers	*Leaders*	*Workers*	*Total*
Maxion	Brazil	5	5	11	21
	China	9	4	16	29
GE	Brazil	1	1	18	20
	China	1	9	38	48
Total		**16**	**19**	**83**	**118**

In order to have a better Knowledge Sharing among Workers, based on the established scale, indicate the relative importance of the following alternatives:

Conversation among workers	9	7	5	3	1	3	5	7	9	Write Standard Operating Procedures (SOP)
Write Standard Operating Procedures (SOP)	9	7	5	3	1	3	5	7	9	Study Standard Operating Procedures (SOP)

Saaty's Scale (1988): Same importance (1); Low importance (3); Middle importance (5); High importance (7); and Extreme importance (9).

Figure 5.2 Sample question of pairwise comparison of factors

among workers (socialization) is of extreme importance (the maximum value 9 in the matrix) in comparison to writing SOPs (externalization). Once all factors were compared, the geometric mean[1] of the matrix (fifth column of the table) as well as the arithmetic mean[2] of each column (fifth row of the table) were calculated, which makes it possible to calculate the relative priorities of each factor in its normalized form (sixth column of the table). As highlighted in the matrices (Table 5.2), the grey values correspond to the responses to parity comparisons acquired during the survey. The other values above the main diagonal were deduced according to the method used, and the values entered below the main diagonal correspond to the reciprocal (inverse) values of those above the main diagonal. For the other judgments regarding the alternatives in relation to the three criteria, the same decisions were made, with $\lambda = 12$ and Consistency Index = 0. The priority importance column indicates that conversation among operators – socialization (89.01%) appears to be viewed as the most important factor by Respondent A.

In order to obtain more insights from the AHP findings, we conducted interviews with some senior employees (Table 5.3) who worked in Brazil and/or China plants to share and discuss the IPC-AHP results (Table 5.4). We extracted condensed meaning unit from the answers (Stemler, 2000) to generate a better understanding of the differences about worker knowledge

Table 5.2 Example of incomplete pairwise comparison

Respondent A	*Conversation among Workers*	*Write Standard Operating Procedures*	*Study Standard Operating Procedures*	*Geometric Average*	*Priority of Importance (%)*
Conversation among workers	1	9	81	9.00	89.01
Write standard operating procedures	1/9	1	9	1.00	9.89
Study standard operating procedures	0	1/9	1	0.11	1.10
Total				10.11	100.0

Table 5.3 Profile of interviewees

Respondents			*Experience (Years)*		
Job function (CODE)	*Birthplace*	*Plant*	*Industrial*	*Chinese plant*	*Brazilian plant*
Engineering manager (EMB)	Brazil	Maxion Brazil	35	1	34
Process engineer (PEB)	Brazil	Maxion Brazil	20	1	19
Engineering supervisor (PSC)	China	Maxion China	20	13	0
Production leader (GPB)	Brazil	Maxion Brazil	20	0	20
Engineering manager (MGD)	Brazil	GE Brazil	20	6	14
Plant manager (MGS)	China	GE China	11	11	0
Advanced manuf. manager (MGM)	Brazil	GE Brazil	11	0	11

sharing in both countries (see Appendix in Chapter 4). These interviews lasted around 60 minutes.

Findings

Maxion Wheels

Maxion China production plant workers consider Internalization – study the SOP (51.8%) as the most relevant knowledge conversion process for better knowledge sharing among workers (Table 5.4), which is indicated by its three hierarchical levels, blue-collars worker (46.9%), production leader (62.70%) and manager (46.9%). Maxion Brazil plant workers indicate Socialization – dialogue among workers (48.3%) as most important for better knowledge sharing among workers, which is highlighted by production leaders (60.3%) and workers (68.2%).

In relation to tacit knowledge, it can be said that it is rooted in individual action, in experiences, ideas and values. The nature of tacit knowledge suggests that communication and language are not enough to share and use certain knowledge, even when it is understood. Externalization is triggered by dialogue or collective reflection.

Incentive (19.9%) stood out among respondents from both Maxion plants in China (17.7%) and Brazil (22.5%). The respondents considered the incentive as the most relevant factor as well as Brazilian workers (39.6%). Brazilian managers indicated training (23.3%), objectives (17.9%) and communication (15.7%) as more relevant than incentives (3.6%).

Chinese managers, production leaders and operators consider problem-solving method (13.7%) and SOP (11.7%) as relevant factors. Among Chinese managers, SOP (20.3%) stood out among the process factors, which supported

Table 5.4 AHP data summary (Maxion)

Enabling factors			*Aggregating individual judgment by geometric means (%)*								*Overall aggregation by arithmetic means (%)*
			Maxion Brazil			*Maxion China*			*Maxion Brazil*	*Maxion China*	*Maxion*
			WC	*LD*	*BC*	*WC*	*LD*	*BC*			
Criteria		SOC	7.0	60.3	68.2	20.3	25.8	25.9	48.3	24.3	36.3
		EXT	14.3	9.5	14.8	32.8	11.5	23.3	16.6	23.8	20.2
		INT	78.8	30.1	17.0	46.9	62.7	50.9	35.2	51.8	43.5
Alternatives	*People*	OBJ	17.9	8.9	0.4	4.2	8.5	6.6	2.6	5.3	4.0
		STR	6.4	3.3	0.4	1.6	10.0	5.3	1.4	3.7	2.5
		COM	15.7	8.7	1.0	3.1	8.2	10.9	4.2	7.5	5.8
		TRA	23.3	5.2	2.8	3.8	5.7	7.5	6.0	6.5	6.3
		PC	4.2	7.7	1.6	2.2	3.0	2.6	3.3	2.8	3.0
		PR	7.1	21.1	1.8	2.8	4.0	3.7	6.5	3.7	5.1
		INC	3.6	9.3	39.6	17.7	9.2	17.5	22.5	17.3	19.9
	Process	PSM	6.2	9.1	3.5	13.2	19.0	11.6	7.9	13.7	10.8
		SOP	10.2	11.2	4.2	20.3	12.9	7.4	10.7	11.7	11.2
		5S	2.7	4.1	11.3	14.6	7.6	7.1	11.1	9.4	10.3
		ZD	1.8	9.2	21.0	6.7	5.4	7.3	16.8	7.2	12.0
		QC	0.9	2.3	12.5	9.6	6.6	12.6	7.1	11.1	9.1
RESP#			5	5	11	9	4	16	21	29	50

WC = White-collar, LD = Leader, BC = Blue-collar, SOC = Socialization, EXT = Externalization, INT = Internalization, OBJ = Objective, STR = Structure, COM = Communication, TRA = Training, PC = Personal Characteristics, PR = Personal Relationship, INC = Incentive, PSM = Problem Solution Methods, SOP = Standard Operating Procedure, ZD = Zero Defect/Mistake-proofing, QC = Quick Changeover internalization (46.9%). 5S (14.6%) was judged as relevant to the Chinese managers respondents too.

In China, the search for better wages, high employment availability and labour laws facilitates high turnover. The Chinese Maxion plant indicated the reasons for relying on internalization to motivate workers to study SOPs in regular bases to remember details of work process: low plant tacit knowledge due to its age (15 years) and high turnover, high variety of wheels produced for a large number of customers, reduction of worker due to the increase of robots, Chinese workers' discipline of following what is specified and losing face for making mistakes.

> For the [Chinese] plant following the instructions indicates professionalism for our customers [Volvo, Daimler, Isuzu…]… achieve specifications from instructions is priority in our plant.
>
> (PSC)

> The Chinese plant have few workers who operate different machines to produce different products for many customers, like Daimler, Isuzu … which require regular reading of work instructions to remember process specifications ….
>
> (PSC)

> I believe a reason for internalization is related to very high turnover [China] …. I have been there twice …. I stayed straight between 2010 to 2011, and when I returned in 2014, I observed that there was almost no one I knew from my first visit …. I would say there were only 20% of people from 2011… that's because there [China] the bureaucracy for changing job [company] is smaller and job availability is higher [than Brazil] … if the worker decides not to go to work tomorrow, he/she asks for a colleague to inform his/her boss [company], or if he gets a job at another company, he starts there immediately … he simply abandons his/her previous job …. Brazil laws requires the employee officially finalizes his/her contract before start in a new company.
>
> (PEB)

> Chinese are much more disciplined than Brazilians …. I usually say, they [Chinese] are very obedient to an order … if you arrive [manager/leader] and tell him to do in a way … he/she will do it exactly in the way explained … if a leader or his boss tells him to follow the instruction … read to learn through this instruction … he/she will do just that.
>
> (PEB)

> For example, the Chinese plant bought a new machine and there was no one who had operated that machine before … how employees learn to operate it? … they study the machine manual … workers are pushed to learn from the material available … procedure … instruction ….
>
> (PEB)

Another interviewee related to internalization by the Chinese referred to losing face. Making mistakes were considered a reason for shame to the Chinese, which contributed to the employees for following instructions with greater discipline and avoiding personal errors.

> The Chinese considers making mistakes a shame [losing face]. They do not like to be reprimanded in public .... In some cases, they hide their mistake which is bad .... They [Chinese] follow the procedures. In case something goes wrong not being warned, as the procedure is the formal guidance to be followed [little freedom to innovate].
>
> (EMB)

In Brazil, socialization (dialogue among operators) prevailed as knowledge conversion process in the judgment of operators and production leaders. Brazilian managers considered internalization (studying SOP) as more relevant to knowledge sharing due to the belief that it created an independence of tacit knowledge. Recording knowledge (know-how) in SOP made it available to different employees, which was a requirement of the standards of quality as ISO 9000.

> In Brazil, the workers are overconfident in their knowledge and experience [tacit knowledge], which makes them less dependent on instructions, but sometimes this brings quality concerns for achieving a specification.
>
> (EMB)

> The manager understands that a detailed and clear instruction allows increasing autonomy and creates a possibility for employees to have multi-task at workstations ... a functional instruction is well done, the plant becomes more flexible when you lose an employee for some reasons [absence or dismissal], ... SOP helps all employees to be able to work in different operations.
>
> (PEB)

However, when questioning the lesser importance of socialization among operators, it was identified that there was a recognition of its importance for sharing tacit knowledge and improving the instructions themselves. Even though its value from a managerial point of view was lower, it was still recognized as relevant.

> Internalization is very important ... dialogue [socialization] is less important but necessary [socialization].
>
> (PSC)

> So, I think .... Brazilian workers find dialogue between them the easiest way to transfer knowledge ... more than reading an instruction ....
>
> (PEB)

> I believe that instruction can be improved by talking to experienced operators [dialogue among operators] ... their experience on the shop floor is essential, so that you can get accurate information ... and share it from operator A to operator B. I think this does not only occur through an instruction, I think that the conversation contributes a lot ... there are companies that have a culture of quick conversation when changing shifts ... to explain what happened during that shift. I think the conversation [socialization] is fundamental ... it is important.
>
> (PEB)

All Chinese employees have been using an internal communication application (ICA) for connecting people [i.e., *WhatsApp*, *Telegram*], which is assumed to minimize internalization, but due to *mianzi* and discipline in following instructions, it did not increase socialization substantially. Currently, the problem-solving method (PDCA) has encouraged a greater verbal exposure by workers.

> We use the ICA [app] to communicate at the plant most of the time. There is also an app to support problem solving method, and it can be used remotely and in person to record the data and steps of the given problem solution providing a history without paper.
>
> (PSC)

> When an employee there [Chinese plant] presents a solution to a problem, you could see his pride ... because many of them started in the plant with no industrial experience [they used to work in agriculture].
>
> (EMB)

The Brazilian plant has accumulated more knowledge and experience about the processes, has low turnover and is located in a small country town where it is the main employer. Knowledge sharing has been done by several generations of workers.

> I think the difference among them [Chinese] and us here in Brazil is that as a mature plant, knowledge has been passing through employee over the years ... we have three to four generations of people from the same family still working in the company, so it is natural to pass knowledge from generations to generations ... in the newest Chinese Maxion plant, this does not happen because no one learned from experienced employees ... they learned through the equipment manual, literature, training, ...
>
> (PEB)

> ... in the Brazilian plant .... a lot of this knowledge is in the employees' minds [tacit knowledge] ... here today many of them have been working in the company for more than 30–35 years .... so, this knowledge is much more inside people's heads than in the instructions.
>
> (PEB)

> Our operators [Brazilian plant] have been working for a long time. A lot of time in their role ... so most of them, because they have a lot of experience, do not study the instructions ... in many cases they participated in its elaboration.
>
> (PLB)

It is observed that there is a similarity on the shop floor context and treatment over workers with routine activities, pressures to meet production volumes and the same incentive practices, which highlight wage increase as relevant for workers.

> In indirect activities to support production, other factors contribute to the professionals for feeling happy, work environment, relationship with the manager, workload ... on the plant floor, pressure on production targets is common in all companies .... I think that for operators what is important is to earn more money [different since the work context is always similar], regardless of the process .... Wherever they [production employees] are going to be there under pressure .... So, what makes them [operators] different is whether they are earning more or less.
>
> (PEB)

> When we talk about incentives, we are talking about salary increase ... I think that in China the incentive is to get a better salary ... here in Brazil too.
>
> (PEB)

> The incentive for the operator is salary increase, which motivates him to feel being valued. He ends up trying harder for what is asked of him. They understand that they are looking at his side [recognition].
>
> (PLB)

A Chinese cultural characteristic is that the man is the family's breadwinner, which, in the context of a one-child family, generates a greater obligation on the male operator to provide better comforts to his family and is a reason for their search for better wages. The Chinese plant has managed this factor through financial gains by meeting challenging targets.

> Most operators are men and they are responsible for providing more comfort to their family. That is why money is important ... to avoid impacts on costs we negotiated some challenging targets for the year linked to a financial gain.
>
> (PSC)

> Society in China is paternalistic ... the eldest son takes care of his entire family. Usually, they all live together ... grandparents, parents and children.
>
> (EMB)

Brazilian managers indicated that factors, such as training, objectives and communication as relevant rather than incentives. However, it should be noted that this is seen by them as an increase in cost, and a factor that is difficult to manage when treated in a personalized manner.

> Managers tend to want workers to share knowledge without financial rewards. Hence, I indicate training and other factors as relevant for knowledge sharing, because if you think that the operators will only share knowledge for financial gains. The manager becomes a hostage of an individual negotiation.
>
> (PEB)

Production leaders train direct operators. However, some leaders, like 2nd (night shift), do not have direct contacts with the technicians who prepare the engineering changes and therefore lose the relevant information to train their team.

> Training is important, but on the shop floor training is still done by the line leader … operators must receive training for every engineering change [revised SOP] but we leaders are not trained to do it [2nd and 3rd shift].
>
> (PLB)

Production leaders in Brazil, experienced operators who stood out to be responsible for the work team, have direct contacts with the operators and considered the personal relationship (21.07%) as a relevant factor. Continuous improvement context promotes greater engagement of operators in decisions related to processes. In this sense, interpersonal relationships influence the sharing of knowledge. Personal relationships influence communication and socialization.

> I realize that today's employees [Brazil] are responding better when there is a good relationship with their manager … it was the time when employees were frightened by their boss … and feared him for fear of losing their job …. I understand that more and more employees are in line with the rules in terms of how a relationship is established between them and their manager.
>
> (PEB)

> The personal relationship is important because most of the time knowledge is passed on between people. For example, it [knowledge] is passed on from more experienced operator to less experienced one, who accompanies him in daily activities until he performs his tasks properly. So having a good relationship helps to make it work.
>
> (PLB)

> Communication is as important as personal relationships. If you pass the problem onto the operators and there is a good dialogue [relationship/socialization], they will help to solve the problem.
>
> (PLB)

The results in China indicated an appreciation of the structure (10.01%) by the production leaders. The analysis of interviews showed a relationship among structure, roles and responsibilities of employees and access to material and financial resources, and Chinese discipline with a strong willingness to follow agreed rules and plans. When there were deviations regarding the planned results, there is little engagement of the individuals for recovery through actions that are not their responsibility. For example, not meeting an expected production volume due to lack of labour or equipment breakdown is not seen as a problem for the production leader from his perspective. Among Brazilian production leaders, there was a greater effort to creatively negotiate alternatives to solve a given problem than the Chinese. It was observed that among Brazilian employees, the failure to meet a goal that was being collectively pursued represented an example of losing face.

> The Chinese are very disciplined, so if you set up a production line support structure that works with three employees in an operation to produce 1500 wheels, and in a given situation [lack, dismissal] the leader only has two of them and produces 800, the leader says I lost resource I cannot do anything else .... I did my part. Here in Brazil, you are normally required to react in some way to meet the agreed targets [losing face].
>
> (PEB)

Regarding the role of Communication (10.89%), its importance was indicated in view of the type of production process of the two factories, the machines of which needed constant parameter adjustments by production support professionals external to the manufacturing line, which was based on communications between line and support area employees.

> Certainly [the relevance of the communication] is due to the characteristic of the process equipment that we have ... both here [Brazil] and in China ... you go on the line to see a problem and you always have to readjust a parameter because it just happened ... maintenance, ... new device ... material ... what is not foreseen in the instructions ....
>
> (PEB)

It was identified that the alternatives were treated in a contingent way, a given demand such as the problem-solving method to be encouraged by a director, or greater attention to 5S due to a customer's requirement influences the valuation of production factors. This can occur in the factors of people and knowledge, but the discussion of the results indicated its coherence related to the characteristics of workers in each plant.

> We had a low performance in the evaluation of client M regarding 5S, so we are working better on this issue ....
>
> (PSC)

Quick changeover is valued by Chinese operators who are adapting to work on multiple machines and benefit from this factor, so that the machine produces faster after changing the product. The Chinese plant increases managerial best practices in the search for greater competitiveness through quality and productivity, for example, the adoption of the Toyota Production System.

> When I was in the Chinese plant, I did not see the kaizen/lean concepts applied [2010-2014] … recently other colleagues went there to buy Chinese tooling service. They told me something different from what I witnessed … they visited several suppliers to select one for a certain project here at the plant …. and they made excellent comments about all these suppliers … saying that companies are no longer concerned about manufacturing for manufacturing …. they already talk a lot about quality and the Japanese model [Toyota Production system] that is there in their side … they [Chinese] are already starting to enter into the automaker's with their products [higher product quality requirement], before they were focused on the aftermarket [lower product quality requirement] … my colleagues said that the companies there are fully organized with the latest technology and they pay attention to sharing knowledge among all employees … mainly because of practices like Kaizen … where you exchange a lot of experience ….
>
> (PEB)

> There were five visits being scheduled to check the service progress to be delivered and only two were made as they were surprised by what they found there … the service was delivered on schedule under a satisfactory level of quality ….
>
> (PEB)

The Chinese plant has valued the use of problem-solving method, which has been encouraged by the management there, and the increasing use of the practice of training by more experienced operators was also cited, which is a form of socialization.

> We need operators to work on multiple processes, so we've had the most experienced operators to train the newest ones ….
>
> (PSC)

GE Hydro

The interviews with the managers reveal the cultural differences between Brazilian and Chinese employees who influence knowledge sharing on the shop floor. The blue- and white-collars workers data about knowledge, process and people factors indicate that at the Brazilian GE Hydro plant (Table 5.5), managers and workers considered the importance of dialogue among workers – socialization for GE Brazilian plant (56.3%). The Chinese plant indicated

Table 5.5 AHP data summary (GE Hydro)

Enabling factors			*Aggregating individual judgment by geometric means (%)*								*Overall aggregation by arithmetic means (%)*
			GE Brazil			*GE China*			*GE Brazil*	*GE China*	*GE*
			WC	*LD*	*BC*	*WC*	*LD*	*BC*			
Criteria		SOC	85.6	1.1	56.5	42.9	13.1	23.9	56.3	21.9	39.1
		EXT	12.3	9.9	33.2	14.3	26.1	34.0	31.8	31.4	31.6
		INT	1.8	89.0	10.3	42.9	60.8	42.1	11.9	46.6	29.3
Alternatives	*People*	OBJ	0.4	0.3	0.2	8.5	7.1	7.2	0.3	7.6	4.0
		STR	3.7	2.3	0.2	1.5	1.9	2.1	2.4	1.9	2.2
		COM	1.3	0.5	0.4	8.5	3.6	6.5	0.7	6.2	3.5
		TRA	9.5	3.5	1.3	11.6	6.7	5.8	4.8	8.1	6.5
		PC	5.4	1.3	2.5	5.1	4.8	4.3	0.9	4.1	2.5
		PR	1.1	0.6	1.2	3.2	5.9	3.2	3.1	4.7	3.9
		INC	9.9	32.2	51.8	14.9	12.4	19.2	31.3	15.5	23.4
	Process	PSM	1.1	0.2	4.4	25.4	13.5	10.7	1.9	16.5	9.2
		SOP	7.5	0.9	7.6	14.9	18.3	9.4	5.4	14.2	9.8
		5S	1.1	6.4	4.5	3.0	8.1	9.0	4.0	6.7	5.4
		ZD	9.1	45.2	15.1	0.6	7.6	11.7	23.1	6.6	14.9
		QC	50.0	6.5	10.8	3.0	10.1	10.9	22.4	8.0	15.2
RESP#			1	1	18	1	9	38	20	48	68

WC = White-collar, LD = Leader, BC = Blue-collar, SOC = Socialization, EXT = Externalization, INT = Internalization, OBJ = Objective, STR = Structure, COM = Communication, TRA = Training, PC = Personal Characteristics, PR = Personal Relationship, INC = Incentive, PSM = Problem Solution Methods, SOP = Standard Operating Procedure, ZD = Zero Defect/Mistake-proofing, QC = Quick Changeover internalization (46.6%) as most important, and manager (42.9%), production leaders (60.8%) and workers (42.1%) respondents indicated their strong preference for internalization.

The importance of incentive in the knowledge sharing process is highlighted in the judgment of respondents from both GE plants. The Brazilian plant has more experience with the processes, and respondents indicate error proofing and quick changeover as more important, which influence the productivity of the processes. The Chinese plant indicates problem-solving method and SOP as the most relevant to knowledge sharing, indicating concern with process learning and task standardization. The concern with learning is indicated by the managers who emphasize the training factor (11.6%).

In both plants, knowledge sharing is based on experienced workers supporting novices, but tacit knowledge is only effectively shared within a favourable organizational context, or Ba, among workers to overcome the cultural differences, such as strong sense of belonging and social harmony in which a climate of trust and openness is presented (Nakano et al., 2013). According to Polanyi (2009), people learn more when they do it. Workers in these production lines develop tacit skills and knowledge that are important for supply chain, and this knowledge is harder to share when compared to explicit knowledge because of its subjective character and how it can be shared (McInerney, 2013).

Managers and workers at Brazilian GE Hydro plant consider importance of dialogue among workers – socialization for GE Brazilian plant (56.3%). At GE Chinese plant, managers, production leaders and workers consider study the SOPs – internalization (46.6%), as more relevant, and externalization in both plants have similar values.

> In Brazil, I see a strong alignment between managers and workers … they prefer to talk to each other to share the knowledge, and in China, I see some differences.
>
> (MGS)

Brazilians' workers prefer to share their knowledge through socialization, teamwork, dialogue and share tacit knowledge among colleagues.

> We, Brazilians, like it a lot, when someone asks how do you do that? and the other one explains.
>
> (MGM)

> The Brazilian workers … have an easy relationship; the employee may be incentivized to teach others.
>
> (MGM)

> Today Brazilian workers learn by talking. All operators pass through formal internal training, and a lot of learning is socialized during hands on tasks.
>
> (MGM)

> The Brazilian worker, I think, is a guy who prefers talking. He is not very formal, but more informal.
>
> (MGD)

Chinese workers are more work-focused, disciplined and look for a better understanding about their tasks through SOPs. It is interesting to observe that the Chinese plant workers have less experience than the Brazilian plant workers. Institutional documents are a relevant source of knowledge for the Chinese, and Brazilian workers like to share their knowledge through socialization, group work and conversations among workers to share tacit knowledge among their colleagues.

> The Chinese workers are proactive, like to learn and have no time constraint to work … the problem is that the Chinese do not like to pass knowledge to each other for fear of losing their job, so it is difficult to work as a team with them.
>
> (MGD)

> The Chinese valued more studying too … the values of the Chinese worker [socialization, internalization, externalization] were closer than that of the Brazilian worker. There was less dispersion … anyway. The Chinese leaders are managing to align themselves more with their workers, passing their concern of following the rules [SOP]. I think the Chinese leader manages to have more influence on the behaviors of the workers.
>
> (MGD)

> Usually, Chinese understands that they will assimilate information better and know what he must do by following what the official document is saying. So Chinese is influenced by the cultural axiom of 'I follow what is written, what is written I follow'.
>
> (MGM)

> Production leaders directly manage the workers on the shop floor. He thinks that employees need to read and be aware of the process sheets, instructions, drawings, quality instructions, every official document related to their tasks [internalization/study].
>
> (MGM)

> I think the leader is looking for more respect and to be a little more formal. The leader in both plants is not a direct worker, but he is also not the manager …, He is in transition from worker to manager. He understands the need to be formal and to follow the procedure. When audits indicate they are not following the approved procedures. It is a problem, so I think that explains why the leaders valued studying.
>
> (MGD)

From managers' perspective in Chinese GE plant, socialization and internalization (42.9%) have the same influence in the worker knowledge sharing. In the managers' assessment, workers could improve socialization and internalization by learning the instruction and sharing the information with each other.

From Chinese production leaders' perspective, internalization (60.8%) is the most important factor, and then comes externalization and socialization. In the leaders' evaluation, workers could improve internalization to learn faster by reading and understanding the SOP. From workers' perspective in China, internalization (42.1%) is the most important factor, and after that there is externalization and socialization. In the workers' evaluation, they could improve internalization by respecting SOPs.

> For Chinese leaders, I think, it is more related to the cultural aspect, because the leader and the workers work closely on the shop floor. They talk about what have to be done. Usually, Chinese understands that they will assimilate the information better and know what s/he must do by following what the document is saying, so Chinese has cultural aspect of "I follow what is written, what is written I follow".
>
> (MGM)

> I think it is kind of a cultural thing ... like we say new things. Sometimes we [Brazilian] don´t feel ashamed to ask somebody's opinion or how to do it ... we like to learn ... because we want to show I have this ability. I think that is kind of a cultural thing .... I see that the Chinese people want to do it first by themselves and then ask for help from others. So, for me, this is a cultural difference in both countries.
>
> (MGS)

Socialization (85.6%) is considered the most important factor, followed by externalization and internalization from the Brazilian manager being interviewed. In the manager's assessment, workers could improve socialization to learn faster and share information with each other. Quick changeover could bring more productivity and structure follows it. Brazilian production leader considers internalization (89.0%) as the most important factor, followed by externalization and socialization. In the leader's assessment, workers could improve Internalization to learn faster reading and understanding the instruction.

From workers' perspective in Brazil, socialization (56.5%) is the most important factor, followed by externalization (33.2%) and internalization (10.3%). In the worker's assessment, workers could improve socialization to learn faster and share information each other. Incentive is the most important factor and could bring more productivity.

> I see the workers [Brazilian] coming through the assembly line many times and saying, "how do you do this or that?" and other employee explain, "Oh, this does this way". Brazilian workers signalled this part of socialization ....
>
> (MGM)

> The Brazilian worker gives more value to speaking, I mean, you see that the worker is aligned with the manager … but I think the leader is looking forward to become a little more professional [previously he used to be worker], to leave informality, to be a little more formal [because this the socialization was not assessed with higher value].
>
> (MGD)

The highest value given to people factor from both Brazilian and Chinese respondents was the incentive, which the interviewees referred to the American culture on financial incentive to achieve competitiveness and recognize meritocracy among workers.

> We have a skill matrix within the organization. In the plant, you have from level 1 to level 4. According to knowledge and behaviour you say, 'this guy has skill level 1, this one has level 2, 3 and 4' and highest level means you become a senior, a facilitator of knowledge sharing. The higher you go up in this skill matrix and consequently, the more you will increase your salary, increasing your positioning and your level within the organization.
>
> (MGM)

The interviews indicated other reasons why internalization prevails in GE Chinese plant, including the influence of European engineering, less human-orientation and more performance orientation (formality) and the short tenure of the Chinese plant with a workforce having less experience than the Brazilian.

> We [Brazilians] are not very formal in terms of writing paper and procedure. We value person - person contact. I think this is a similarity between Brazil and China. That is why I think that both the China manager and the Brazil manager valued speaking to transmit knowledge.
>
> (MGD)

> China receives a lot of input about hydro engineering from Europe where is the export market from the Chinese product; The European culture, which is a little more formal for China, continues to influence China, so that is why there is also the part of studying for the Chinese manager. This must be influenced by the pressure from Europe, the incentive that Europe keeps on doing so that they have every procedure being documented.
>
> (MGD)

> I think the procedural focus [study/internalization] is specially related to new workers. You can imagine if we have the workers working together for more than three to five years, some problems will occur when they talk to each other. I think that is [internalization] more specific for new workers.
>
> (MGS)

> The answers are related to the desire that employee would also need more talking among themselves. They obviously believe that studying is important, but dialogues and everything else would be an important form of knowledge sharing. I think that if you do this research today in China, it would be very similar. The manager who is there today, should be very similar to this result.
>
> (MGM)

Chinese respondents highlighted knowledge sharing was related to process factor, such as problem-solving method and work instruction. Otherwise, the actions with quick changeover and error proofing that take more working in groups and with higher degree of socialization, presented higher percentage among the Brazilian respondents.

The incentive factor receives the highest score from both Brazilian and Chinese respondents, which shows that the cultural value of emphasizing financial incentive to workers has been absorbed in both units and is a unanimous point regarding the way to achieve competitiveness and meritocracy.

> I think they recognize that this is important. The personal contact between the leader and the workers is the main lever to be able to motivate people. And this can be seen in the form of a compliment, an orientation, having a cup of coffee together and feeling close to the person. But the training appeared there, which we had already mentioned before. In China there is a lot of training and is more than here. It is very common to have training outside, or inside our plant.
>
> (MGD)

> For us, the manufacturing training is always an important thing, because we need to have the worker to know all the requirements and procedures, right? So, training would be the first step to bring them into his stage.
>
> (MGS)

The most internalized indications for knowledge sharing are highlighted by Chinese respondents, such as problem-solving method and work instruction. Otherwise, the actions with quick changeover and zero defect have more group work and a higher degree of socialization presented higher percentage among the Brazilian respondents.

> I think that the perception of being "quick change" among managers and workers is because one is thinking about financial result and other is thinking about agility of their work, and more or less there is a priority. The issue of error proofing is due to the scenario that really, if I have a system that does not allow me to cause a defect, it has to be a priority.
>
> (MGM)

> The right work instruction will be the most important think for the workers. Because all of them will follow the work instruction, right? If the work instruction is good and can be delivered with good quality, it means that the worker has less opportunities to make a mistake. And we can have a good result in terms of Environmental, Health and Safety (EHS), quality and operation, right? So, I think that's why, especially for the manager and the leaders, I think these two levers are most important.
>
> (MGS)

Some people and process factors influence the socialization and internalization conversion process. Incentive is relevant for workers' knowledge sharing among Brazilian and Chinese respondents, which shows that promoting financial incentive to workers influences knowledge sharing.

> I think they [Chinese] recognize that human contacts between the leader and the workers support incentive, and this can influence knowledge sharing (i.e. chat, a cup of tea together …).
>
> (MGM)

The internalization of knowledge is highlighted by Chinese respondents, such as problem-solving method and work instruction. Otherwise, the actions with quick changeover and zero defect that take more working in group and a higher degree of socialization presented higher percentage among the Brazilian respondents.

> I think that managers and workers indicate quick changeover technique as relevant because it impacts financial and agility of their work … error proofing mitigates quality issues.
>
> (MGM)

Conclusion

The results from both AHP and qualitative interviews reveal the cross-cultural influence on knowledge sharing from the perspectives of managers, production leaders and workers. While the Chinese blue-collar workers prefer to share knowledge through internalization (study written procedures), respecting the hierarchy in a disciplined manner, the Brazilian workers prefer to share knowledge through socialization, teamwork and conversations between peers to share his/her tacit knowledge among the colleagues. Some enabling factors of knowledge sharing, such as incentive, are also highlighted by the interviewees in both Brazilian and Chinese production plants under study. In particular, there is an open dialogue between managers and workers in Brazilian plant. But Chinese culture of avoiding losing face and fear of making mistakes prohibit greater communication between people.

In China, Internalization (studying instructions) is more relevant, partly because of the culture that values discipline, obedience to orders, fear of error [losing face], partly because of the organizational part than having a worker dealing with a wide variety of products and having less experience than Brazilians need the instructions to remember the specifications. By following the instructions, the Chinese employee reduces the risk of errors but restricts suggestions for improvement, which begin to be encouraged by managers.

The Brazilian factory accumulates greater experience in the production of wheels. The current culture of continuous improvement values greater dialogue between hierarchical levels and proposals for improvements. In this sense, employees are more exposed and share more knowledge through socialization (dialogue about instructions). Respondents indicate financial incentive as an important factor for knowledge sharing. In China, this comes from the tradition of the man being the provider of the family and as there are several cases of being the only child, the search for higher remuneration contributes to providing better conditions for your family members.

Notes

1 Each plant results use means based on the *Aggregating individual Judgment – AIJ method* (Ramanathan & Ganesh, 1994; Saaty, 1988) and considers aggregation of data from the same organization to represent the plant/white- or blue-collar judgment (i.e., Global Priorities and/or Overall Results of white and/or blue collar from the same plant separately).

2 Overall Aggregation uses arithmetic means based on the *Aggregating Individual Priorities – AIP method* (Forman & Peniwati, 1998; Ishizaka & Nemery, 2013) and considers aggregation of all judgments to consolidate the results (i.e., overall Aggregation of white- and/or blue-collar employees from the 4 plants researched, and consolidate the 4 plants data to the sector result).

References

Alcântara, M. B. S. A. (2021). Cultura e Gestão do Conhecimento: um estudo comparativo em fábricas de rodas no Brasil e na China [Portuguese]; Culture and knowledge management: A comparative study of wheel factories in Brazil and China [Master's thesis]. School of Engineering of Guaratingueta, Sao Paulo State University, UNESP Repository.

Ardichvili, A., Jondle, D., Kowske, B., Cornachione, E., Li, J., & Thakadipuram, T. (2012). Ethical cultures in large business organizations in Brazil, Russia, India, and China. *Journal of Business Ethics*, *105*(4), 415–428.

Ardichvili, A., Maurer, M., Li, W., Wentling, T., & Stuedemann, R. (2006). Cultural influences on knowledge sharing through online communities of practice. *Journal of Knowledge Management*, *10*(1), 94–107.

Costilhas, A. A. M. (2020). Workers knowledge sharing improvements and the cultural influence: Comparative study Brazil and China in a capital good industry [Master's thesis]. School of Engineering of Guaratingueta, Sao Paulo State University, Unesp Repository: https://repositorio.unesp.br/handle/11449/202394

Erden, Z., Von Krogh, G., & Nonaka, I. (2008). The quality of group tacit knowledge. *The Journal of Strategic Information Systems*, *17*(1), 4–18.

Forman, E., & Peniwati, K. (1998). Aggregating individual judgements and priorities with the analytic hierarchy process. *European Journal of Operational Research*, *108*(1), 165–169.

Goswami, A. K., Agrawal, R. K., & Goswami, M. (2021). Influence of national culture on knowledge management process: Literature review and research agenda. *Benchmarking: An International Journal*, *28*(4), 1186–1212.

Harker, P. T. (1987). Incomplete pairwise comparisons in the analytic hierarchy process. *Mathematical Modelling*, *9*(11), 837–848.

Hong, J. F., Snell, R. S., & Easterby-Smith, M. (2006). Cross-cultural influences on organizational learning in MNCS: The case of Japanese companies in China. *Journal of International Management*, *12*(4), 408–429.

Hu, S. J., Ko, J., Weyand, L., Elmaraghy, H. A., Lien, T. K., Koren, Y., Bley, H., Chryssolouris, G., Nasr, N., & Shpitalni, M. (2011). Assembly system design and operations for product variety. *CIRP Annals – Manufacturing Technology*, *60*(2), 715–733.

Ishizaka, A., & Nemery, P. (2013). *Multi-criteria decision analysis: Methods and software*. John Wiley & Sons.

Kotha, S. (1995). Mass customization: Implementing the emerging paradigm for competitive advantage. *Strategic Management Journal*, *16*(S1), 21–42.

McInerney, D. M. (2013). *Educational psychology: Constructing learning*. Pearson Higher Education AU.

Muniz, J., Jr., Batista, E. D., Jr., & Loureiro, G. (2010a). Knowledge-based integrated production management model applied to automotive companies. *International Journal of Knowledge Management Studies*, *4*(3), 301–318.

Muniz, J., Jr., Batista, E. D., Jr., & Loureiro, G. (2010b). Knowledge-based integrated production management model. *Journal of Knowledge Management*, *14*(6), 858–871.

Muniz, J., Jr., Hong, J., Oliveira, S., Wintersberger, D., & Popadiuk, S. (2019). Knowledge sharing in the automotive sector: A comparative study of Chinese and Brazilian firms. *Production*, *29*(1), 1–21.

Muniz, J., Jr., Ribeiro, V. B., & Pradhan, N. (2021). Knowledge-based assessment applied to lean Brazilian Toyota plants: Employees' perceptions. *International Journal of Knowledge Management*, *17*(2), 1–22.

Muniz, J., Jr., Wintersberger, D., & Hong, J. L. (2021). Worker and manager judgments about factors that facilitate knowledge-sharing: Insights from a Brazilian automotive assembly line. *Knowledge and Process Management* (early view). doi: 10.1002/kpm.1693

Nakano, D., Muniz, J., Jr., & Batista, E. D., Jr. (2013). Engaging environments: Tacit knowledge sharing on the shop floor. *Journal of Knowledge Management*, *17*(2), 290–306.

Polanyi, M. (2009). *The tacit dimension*. University of Chicago Press.

Ramanathan, R., & Ganesh, L. S. (1994). Group preference aggregation methods employed in AHP: An evaluation and an intrinsic process for deriving members' weightages. *European Journal of Operational Research*, *79*(2), 249–265.

Saaty, T. L. (1988). What is the analytic hierarchy process? In *Mathematical models for decision support* (pp. 109–121). Springer.

Stemler, S. (2000). An overview of content analysis. *Practical Assessment, Research, and Evaluation*, *7*(1), 17.

6 Concluding Remarks

Summary

Our study aims to identify the cultural-specific factors affecting the knowledge sharing activities among production workers and associated challenges encountered by foreign subsidiaries of MNCs in Brazil and China. By adopting a mixed method with a combination of qualitative case studies (GE Hydro, Maxion Wheels and Toyota Motors) and the Incomplete Pairwise Comparison IPC-AHP (Maxion Wheels and GE Hydro), we are able to reveal a multiplicity of specific cultural factors, namely face and *guanxi* among others, and their corresponding impact on the production workers' knowledge sharing behaviours.

According to our case study findings, both Chinese and Brazilian workers appear to demonstrate significant differences in the following dimensions, including authority, *guanxi*, job security, face and transparency, performance orientation versus humane orientation. While comparing to their Brazilian counterpart, Chinese production workers were found to give a lot of respect to those in authority, devote more time to cultivate *guanxi*, possess higher level of job security and become more sensitive about face-saving.

Drawing on an integrative knowledge management model developed by Muniz et al. (2010a, 2010b), the results from our IPC-AHP analysis further reveal how some specific factors related to people, process and knowledge can affect the effectiveness of socialization, externalization and internalization processes in a production context. Specifically, internalization was the favourite knowledge process mode among Chinese workers, whereas their Brazilian counterparts were found to prefer socialization more. Moreover, incentive was found as the most important factor for both cultures, thus indicating that motivation to engage in knowledge sharing activities remains a critical challenge in cross-cultural context.

Implications for the Rest of the World

Despite the focus of our book is on the cross-cultural influence of knowledge sharing in Brazil and China, the study's implications go beyond these two countries and serve to provide some new insights for both organizational practitioners

DOI: 10.4324/9781003112136-6

and academic researchers in other parts of the world. First, our study challenges the universalistic assumption underpinning the knowledge management practices (Hong et al., 2017). As indicated by the significantly different understandings between Chinese and Brazilian about the appropriate ways for knowledge sharing to occur in a production plant, the MNCs should refrain from adopting any normative 'best practice model' of knowledge management. We suggest to bring back the 'context' in by taking the culturally embedded assumptions and values into consideration when developing a particularistic approach of knowledge management (Glisby & Holden, 2003; Hong et al., 2017). In particular, it is important to identify some key contextual factors that influence the implementation of knowledge management practices, including the indigenous cultural values and assumptions, which is supported by a constuctivist perspective based on result of interaction between people (Nakano, 2006).

Second, managers from developed countries can take note from the experience of how foreign MNCs (i.e., GE, Maxion and Toyota) can overcome the cultural barriers of knowledge sharing in Brazil and China, respectively. Apart from some commonly identified work-related problems, such as frontline workers' passivity and reluctance to undertake responsibility and their deference to upper authorities for decision-making, indigenous cultural values will also undermine the effectiveness of knowledge sharing, thus creating some pressures for local adaptation. In this regard, other foreign MNCs should identify some salient cultural dimensions underpinning their model of knowledge management and their potential variations abroad. Without such understanding, it is difficult to evaluate how these cultural differences might impinge upon the transferability of knowledge management in particular national contexts.

Third, managers located in developing countries can also have a better understanding about the cross-cultural challenges from a 'recipient' perspective. Given the fact that knowledge sharing involves two-way interactions and local managers are usually the ones to receive foreign knowledge, there requires an on-going experimentation at local context in order to cross the cultural boundaries for harnessing their location-specific insights. Those 'lesson learned' will become part of their knowledge base for future development.

Looking Ahead

The adoption of new technologies in manufacturing, such as cyber-physical systems (CPSs), big data analytics, additive manufacturing, Internet of things (IoT), artificial intelligence, robotics and cloud computing (Klingenberg et al., 2019; Núñez-Merino et al., 2020), is expected not only to transform the production and the distribution of goods and services. Their adoption has been broadly referred as I4.0 in Germany and Brazil (Drath & Horch, 2014; Lasi et al., 2014), Manufacturing of the Future, Advanced Manufacturing Technology and Smart Factory in the U.S.A. (Chen et al., 2017; Fries et al., 2021; Thomas et al., 2008), Future Manufacturing in the United Kingdom (Mariani & Borghi, 2019; Peters et al., 2016), Digitalization in Germany (Peters et al., 2016) and Smart

Manufacturing in Germany, U.S.A. and Korea (Kang et al., 2016). I4.0 emerged as a new industrial revolution, as new technologies can create intelligent and autonomous systems able to produce customized products in small lots at low costs (Marnewick & Marnewick, 2019; Sony & Naik, 2020; Xu et al., 2018), improve labour conditions by automating repetitive tasks (Karre, 2017), ultimately bringing enhanced organizational performance and fast interaction with customers and suppliers (Abubakar et al., 2019; Schneider, 2018; Szász et al., 2020). Industry practitioners and academia highlight the importance about implementation of I4.0 over manufacturing of goods/services.

We will adopt the term I4.0 to specify the context, which connects suppliers, equipment, plants and corporations digitally in order to create an integrated network and competitive value chain (Li, 2018). I4.0 is directly related to, but not restricted to, the following technologies: CPS, IoT, big data, 3D printing, robotics, simulation, augmented reality, cloud computing and cyber security (Dalenogare et al., 2018; Fernández-Caramés & Fraga-Lamas, 2018; Yang & Gu, 2021). Specific examples of skills required for these technological domains are shown in Table 6.1.

I4.0 technologies enable the manufacturing plants to cope with learning and decision-making in real time, which is supported by dedicated high performance networks (CPS) to facilitate instantaneous data communication between machines and processes on the assembly line (Zezulka et al., 2016). The dynamic integration promoted by CPS is capable to collaborate with planning, analysis, simulation, implementation and maintenance of high-performance manufacturing processes and includes data security (Lu, 2017). It is expected that collaborative robots will be carrying out simultaneous tasks to reduce human interventions on the processes and increase productivity (Wollschlaeger et al., 2017).

Table 6.1 Industry 4.0 technologies and skills requirements

Technological domains	*Skills required*
Big data	Reduce the queuing time inside the same automated working cell with different equipment
Internet of things	Resolve an equipment downtime issue by a maintenance technician offsite
Cyber-physical systems	Collect network delays data that affect productivity
Artificial intelligence	Analyse the decisions made by a machine that would be different by the one made by a production leader, involving programming and statistics
Interoperability	Analyse the proposals from different suppliers for the acquisition of the same hardware and software protocol with a focus on system integration
Programming	Develop a mobile app to mitigate production waste
Information security	Protect corporate data when accessing networks
Collaborative robots	Maximize the output by worker and machines working in the same working cell as a robot in a safe environment
Augmented reality	Provide visual information to support assembling

Source: Nascimento et al. (2022).

The new technologies are expected not only to transform the production process and the distribution of goods and services but also have far-reaching consequences for productivity, skills, environment, income distribution and social well-being (OECD, 2017). The analysis of how different social systems influence the creation, development and implementation of new technologies is fundamental for understanding the dynamics of industrial organizations and the technological changes underway.

Knowledge sharing remains as a critical activity for the organizations under I4.0 since the overall effectiveness and efficiency depends on how well the current know how and best practices can be shared and transferred among members in organizations (Hong et al., 2011). It is a process where people share task relevant ideas, information and suggestions (Eze et al., 2013) among individuals, groups, teams, departments and organizations (Crossan et al., 1999; Ipe, 2003), which is mandatory for new technology implementation.

Currently, assembly line work has become more knowledge intensive, but both in operations management and human resources literature there is a lack of systematic investigation on knowledge sharing from the perspective of assembly line workers (Braverman, 1998; Hu et al., 2011; Muniz et al., 2022). It is often conceived that the successful implementation of a certain technology depends on who applies/uses it, thus neglecting the role of assembly workers who constitute a fundamental element in this process (Di Pasquale et al., 2022; Kipper et al., 2020; Longo et al., 2017). Under I4.0 implementation, there is a need for a skilled worker, including soft skills, such as creativity, problem-solving, communication and networking (Erol et al., 2016; Hecklau et al., 2016; IndustriALL Global Union, 2017; Kaasinen et al., 2020; Kipper et al., 2020; Shamim et al., 2016). The I4.0 requires production operators to gain new skills and cope with challenges of digital transformation. Future research for understanding the impact of the implementation of I4.0 on the workers may contribute to the mitigation of problems related to employment, work and organization and identification of knowledge management practices for the training of workers and supportive HR strategies.

The UN Sustainable Development Goals (SDGs) highlight various aspects related to the need for sustainable industrial transformation (I4.0), especially 'decent work and economic growth (SDG-8)' to promote sustained, inclusive and sustainable economic growth for achieving full and productive employment and decent work for all; and 'Building Resilient Infrastructures (SDG-9)' to promote inclusive and sustainable industrialization and foster innovation; and 'Quality education (SDG-4)' to ensure inclusive, equitable and quality education and promote lifelong learning opportunities for all. From this perspective, it is evident that one of the problems, both in developed and emerging countries, refers to the implementation of I4.0, the challenges of which impose a paradigm changing and innovative conditions for the (re)qualification of workers, since the better the educational system, the better the capacity to adapt to industrial changes and, thus, it can alleviate systemic inequalities. It is also noteworthy that 'Partnerships and Means of Implementation (SDG-17)' declares the need for global cooperation and the establishment of networks to achieve the aforementioned SDGs (IndustriALL Global Union, 2017; Muniz et al., 2022).

I4.0 implementation needs educational methods (Baena et al., 2017), and the complexity associated with existing methods still remains an inhibitor for digital transformation (Erol et al., 2016). Industry 4.0 learning models proposed by Uhlemann et al. (2017), Prinz et al. (2016), Hecklau et al. (2016) and Baena et al. (2017) are highlighted as pioneers, but these methods still require more empirical validation to facilitate the management of development.

HR programmes should be updated to support training strategies in order to prepare workers to handle the I4.0 context (Baena et al., 2017; Prinz et al., 2016; Shamim et al., 2016) driven by mass customization, short life cycle for new products and market volatility. Relevant enablers related to knowledge management on the manufacturing include support and managerial leadership, culture, information technology, strategy and purpose, measurement, organizational infrastructure, processes and activities, motivational incentives, resources, training, human resources management (HRM) practices and personal characteristics (Muniz et al., 2022; Nakano et al., 2013). However, despite the recognition of the factors that enable knowledge sharing in organizations (Muniz et al., 2021; Tohidinia & Mosakhani, 2010; Wang & Noe, 2010), our understanding about the unique challenges encountered by the blue-collar workers in the Industry 4.0 context is rather limited.

Traditionally, production systems vary in terms of variety and volume of output (i.e., assembly lines, manufacturing cells and continuous process), which include people, process and knowledge aspects. We still need to understand the impact of I4.0 on these different productions systems so as to create better strategies of knowledge management. The main research questions related to management of tacit knowledge in Industry 4.0 are:

- Which workers' competencies and skills should be developed (Baena et al., 2017; Prinz et al., 2016; Shamim et al., 2016)?
- Which factors should be considered in HR programmes (Baena et al., 2017; Prinz et al., 2016; Shamim et al., 2016)?
- Which knowledge management strategies may support I4.0 implementation (Burzlaff & Bartelt, 2017; Erol et al., 2016; Radziwon et al., 2014)?

The complexity of new tasks requires flexibility and adaptability from the worker to solve problems and deal with new technologies (Hecklau et al., 2016; Kaasinen et al., 2020; Schneider, 2018). Nascimento et al. (2022) exemplify employees' soft-skills (Table 6.2), which is relevant in this scenario of I4.0 implementation. Sié and Yakhlef (2009) highlight that knowledge sharing and learning depend on people and occur through social dialogues to improve worker's judgement and experiences for understanding why things happen.

The implementation of I4.0 has arrived in the subsidiaries of MNCs, which are influenced by cultural aspects in the knowledge acquisition to apply new technologies. Dalenogare et al. (2018) have pointed to some potential difficulties

Table 6.2 Soft skills required for Industry 4.0

Soft skills	*Examples*
Flexibility	Being able to develop yourself outside the companies' daily routine; Work in a manual operation or assisting a collaborative robot
Communication	Made sure that reasons to solve downtime in a specific artificial intelligence app were understood and correctly aligned with the team; interact with a machine developer to understand the scope and benefits of a new CPS industrial computer network
Interpersonal relationships	Being capable of getting a team made up from different areas to solve a complex downtime problem; Being capable to act with IT experts to evolve a continuous improvement program in a computer-integrated production working station
Decision-making	Include IoT specialists to evaluate problem-solving options and select the best solution; attend the command of a production output from an autonomous equipment with artificial intelligence
Pacific coexistence	Being capable of leading people from different ages and backgrounds and launching IoT technology in a workplace with excellent well-being; Being able to share programming knowledge with an experienced worker and deliver the same result
Leadership	Become a listener to understand an IoT problem from maintenance and, together, build the action plan; lead a blue-collar team on how to work in an autonomous integrated equipment aligned with artificial intelligence

Source: Nascimento et al. (2022).

associated with the implementation of new technologies in emerging economies (i.e., performance evaluation, organizational flexibility, worker background, population, age and labour culture). The changing landscape of international competition, accompanied by the rise of multinationals from emerging markets (Williamson & Zeng, 2009), has created a change in thinking among knowledge management scholars in favour of a particularistic approach of researching knowledge sharing (Hong et al., 2017) in different cultural contexts.

In particular, the manufacturing sector of Brazil and China provides a fertile setting for future research providing context-specific cultural and institutional conditions that might impact I4.0 implementation. Currently, both countries have manufacturing processes based on knowledge-intensive and complex nature dependent of worker tacit knowledge. For example, China and Brazil produced over 25.2 million and 2.0 million cars, respectively in 2020 (OICA, 2021), and both countries remain on the ten largest car manufacturers in the world. The automotive industry still represents a significant economic sector in Brazil.

I4.0 will also impact the future job prospects in Brazil and China, since it will demand new professional skills in a new labour context. Other countries such as UK has similarities between China and Brazil because it is investing in developing their own technology as China (Li, 2018) and its unemployment, caused by BREXIT, may represent a context similar compared to Brazil.

The review conducted by Ribeiro et al. (2022) indicate future research pertinent to knowledge management and I4.0 aims to contribute:

- To guide managers how to engage blue-collar workers for digital transformation on the shop floor (Ahmed et al., 2020; Manesh et al., 2021; Muniz et al., 2022);
- To understand how the tacit-explicit knowledge conversion influences knowledge sharing in digital contexts (Thomas, 2020);
- To create a knowledge sharing culture supported by partnership between the employer and the staff, induce cooperation among employees and improve employee's engagement (Ahmed et al., 2020; Benyahya & Matošková, 2021; Ganguly et al., 2019; Manesh et al., 2021; Nakash & Bouhnik, 2021);
- To understand worker behaviours on assembly line, which continue to involve a lot of manual work (Di Pasquale et al., 2022).

The relationship between KM and I4.0 needs be discussed not only from a hard, technology-based perspective, but also from a soft, people-related one. I4.0 implementation demands the identification of critical knowledge for each process. KM can help to integrate technology and people-based aspects and improve skill development, learning and collaboration, IT infrastructure design and product development, and process planning and control (Ribeiro et al., 2022). The review conducted by Ribeiro et al. (2022) highlights three themes to support studies KM and I4.0:

- Technology-based research opportunities are associated with understanding how technologies can influence knowledge creation for operational and strategic applications (i.e., big data);
- KM-related research opportunities are concerned to I4.0 implementation process, which can pose challenges to industries and even countries, as it requires the participation of multiple actors, such as universities and research institutions, government, companies and others;
- Worker's engagement perspective how blue collars engage in learning and knowledge sharing in order to develop new competencies and skills.

Therefore, the topic of knowledge management in Industry 4.0 arouses continued academic interest on the issue of knowledge sharing and stimulates more reflection about the importance of managing workers' tacit knowledge on the shop floor. In this sense, the scenario of reduction of economic activity and layoffs in the industry highlights the importance of effective knowledge sharing, as it influences the remaining employees during their work transformation process and the new hires when the sector becomes stabilized, which should to consider a context of employment, economic growth (SDG-8), equitable and quality education (SDG-4) and inclusive, sustainable industrialization and promoting innovation (SDG-9) in order to avoid social problems.

These research opportunities aim to contribute to create a better social impact of I4.0 with regard to workers' knowledge sharing, sustainable organizational practices in cross-culture contexts. It indicates pragmatic orientations on different ways to identify how the manager can develop favourable contexts to encourage knowledge conversion on the shop floor sharing during I4.0 implementation and identify related factors that influence workers' tacit sharing knowledge in groups.

In conclusion, a better understanding of knowledge, people and process integration will support HRM and contribute to the promotion of a favourable context for the creation and sharing of knowledge by the workers in the Industry 4.0, fostering continuous improvement and broadening the field of vision of the production manager for decision-making and seeking competitiveness.

References

Abubakar, A. M., Elrehail, H., Alatailat, M. A., & Elçi, A. (2019). Knowledge management, decision-making style and organizational performance. *Journal of Innovation & Knowledge*, *4*(2), 104–114.

Ahmed, T., Shahid Khan, M., Thitivesa, D., Siraphatthada, Y., & Phumdara, T. (2020). Impact of employees engagement and knowledge sharing on organizational performance: Study of HR challenges in COVID-19 pandemic. *Human Systems Management*, *39*(4), 589–601.

Baena, F., Guarin, A., Mora, J., Sauza, J., & Retat, S. (2017). Learning factory: The path to Industry 4.0. *Procedia Manufacturing*, *9*, 73–80.

Benyahya, P., & Matošková, J. (2021). Partnership between the employer and the staff as a vital factor for knowledge sharing. *International Journal of Learning and Intellectual Capital*, *18*(1), 5–27.

Braverman, H. (1998). *Labor and monopoly capital: The degradation of work in the twentieth century*. NYU Press.

Burzlaff, F., & Bartelt, C. (2017, April). Knowledge-driven architecture composition: Case-based formalization of integration knowledge to enable automated component coupling. In *2017 IEEE International Conference on Software Architecture Workshops (ICSAW)* (pp. 108–111). IEEE.

Chen, B., Wan, J., Shu, L., Li, P., Mukherjee, M., & Yin, B. (2017). Smart factory of industry 4.0: Key technologies, application case, and challenges. *IEEE Access*, *6*, 6505–6519.

Crossan, M. M., Lane, H. W., & White, R. E. (1999). An organizational learning framework: From intuition to institution. *Academy of Management Review*, *24*, 522–537.

Dalenogare, L. S., Benitez, G. B., Ayala, N. F., & Frank, A. G. (2018). The expected contribution of Industry 4.0 technologies for industrial performance. *International Journal of Production Economics*, *204*, 383–394.

Di Pasquale, V., De Simone, V., Miranda, S., & Riemma, S. (2022). Smart operators: How augmented and virtual technologies are affecting the worker's performance in manufacturing contexts. *Journal of Industrial Engineering and Management*, *15*(2), 233–255.

Drath, R., & Horch, A. (2014). Industrie 4.0: Hit or hype?[industry forum]. *IEEE Industrial Electronics Magazine*, *8*(2), 56–58.

Erol, S., Jäger, A., Hold, P., Ott, K., & Sihn, W. (2016). Tangible Industry 4.0: A scenario-based approach to learning for the future of production. *Procedia CiRp*, *54*, 13–18.

Eze, U. C., Goh, G. G. G., Goh, C. Y., & Tan, T. L. (2013). Perspectives of SMEs on knowledge sharing. *Journal of Information and Knowledge Management Systems, 43*(2), 210–236.

Fernández-Caramés, T. M., & Fraga-Lamas, P. (2018). A review on human-centered IoT-connected smart labels for the Industry 4.0. *IEEE Access, 6*, 25939–25957.

Fries, C., Fechter, M., Nick, G., Szaller, Á., & Bauernhansl, T. (2021). First results of a survey on manufacturing of the future. *Procedia Computer Science, 180*, 142–149.

Ganguly, A., Talukdar, A., & Chatterjee, D. (2019). Evaluating the role of social capital, tacit knowledge sharing, knowledge quality and reciprocity in determining innovation capability of an organization. *Journal of Knowledge Management, 23*(6), 1105–1135.

Glisby, M., & Holden, N. (2003). Contextual constraints in knowledge management theory: The cultural embeddedness of Nonaka's knowledge-creating company. *Knowledge and Process Management, 10*(1), 29–36.

Hecklau, F., Galeitzke, M., Flachs, S., & Kohl, H. (2016). Holistic approach for human resource management in Industry 4.0. *Procedia Cirp, 54*, 1–6.

Hong, J., Snell, R., & Rowley, C. (2017). Asia pacific as a research context for organizational learning: Background and research directions. *Asia Pacific Business Review, 23*(4), 467–474.

Hong, D., Suh, E., & Koo, C. (2011). Developing strategies for overcoming barriers to knowledge sharing based on conversational knowledge management: A case study of a financial company. *Expert Systems with Applications, 38*(12), 14417–14427.

Hu, S. J., Ko, J., Weyand, L., Elmaraghy, H. A., Lien, T. K., Koren, Y., Bley, H., Chryssolouris, G., Nasr, N., & Shpitalni, M. (2011). Assembly system design and operations for product variety. *CIRP Annals – Manufacturing Technology, 60*(2), 715–733.

IndustriALL Global Union. (2017). *The challenge of Industry 4.0 and the demand for new answers*. IndustriALL Global Union. http://www.industriall-union.org/sites/default/files/uploads/documents/2017/SWITZERLAND/Industry4point0Conf/industry_4_en_web.pdf.

Ipe, M. (2003). Knowledge sharing in organizations: A conceptual framework. *Human Resource Development Review, 2*(4), 337–359.

Kaasinen, E., Schmalfuß, F., Özturk, C., Aromaa, S., Boubekeur, M., Heilala, J., & Walter, T. (2020). Empowering and engaging industrial workers with Operator 4.0 solutions. *Computers & Industrial Engineering, 139*, 105678.

Kang, H. S., Lee, J. Y., Choi, S., Kim, H., Park, J. H., Son, J. Y. & Noh, S. D. (2016). Smart manufacturing: Past research, present findings, and future directions. *International Journal of Precision Engineering and Manufacturing-green Technology, 3*(1), 111–128.

Karre, H., Hammer, M., Kleindienst, M., & Ramsauer, C. (2017). Transition towards an Industry 4.0 state of the LeanLab at Graz University of Technology. *Procedia Manufacturing*, 9, 206–213.

Kipper, L. M., Furstenau, L. B., Hoppe, D., Frozza, R., & Iepsen, S. (2020). Scopus scientific mapping production in Industry 4.0 (2011–2018): A bibliometric analysis. *International Journal of Production Research, 58*(6), 1605–1627.

Klingenberg, C. O., Borges, M. A. V., & Antunes Jr, J. A. V. (2019). Industry 4.0 as a data-driven paradigm: A systematic literature review on technologies. *Journal of Manufacturing Technology Management, 32*(3), 570–592.

Lasi, H., Fettke, P., Kemper, H. G., Feld, T., & Hoffmann, M. (2014). Industry 4.0. *Business & Information Systems Engineering, 6*(4), 239–242.

Li, L. (2018). China's manufacturing locus in 2025: With a comparison of "Made-in-China 2025" and "Industry 4.0". *Technological Forecasting and Social Change, 135*, 66–74.

Longo, F., Nicoletti, L., & Padovano, A. (2017). Smart operators in Industry 4.0: A human-centered approach to enhance operators' capabilities and competencies within the new smart factory context. *Computers & Industrial Engineering*, *113*, 144–159.

Lu, Y. (2017). Industry 4.0: A survey on technologies, applications and open research issues. *Journal of Industrial Information Integration*, *6*, 1–10.

Manesh, M. F., Pellegrini, M. M., Marzi, G., & Dabic, M. (2021). Knowledge management in the fourth industrial revolution: Mapping the literature and scoping future avenues. *IEEE Transactions on Engineering Management*, *68*(1), 289–300.

Mariani, M., & Borghi, M. (2019). Industry 4.0: A bibliometric review of its managerial intellectual structure and potential evolution in the service industries. *Technological Forecasting and Social Change*, *149*, 119752.

Marnewick, C., & Marnewick, A. L. (2019). The demands of industry 4.0 on project teams. *IEEE Transactions on Engineering Management*, *67*(3), 941–949.

Muniz, J., Jr., Batista, E. D., Jr., & Loureiro, G. (2010a). Knowledge-based integrated production management model applied to automotive companies. *International Journal of Knowledge Management Studies*, *4*(3), 301–318.

Muniz, J., Jr., Batista, E. D., Jr., & Loureiro, G. (2010b). Knowledge-based integrated production management model. *Journal of Knowledge Management*, *14*(6), 858–871.

Muniz, J., Jr., Ribeiro, V. B., & Pradhan, N. (2021). Knowledge-based assessment applied to lean Brazilian Toyota plants: Employees' perceptions. *International Journal of Knowledge Management*, *17*(2), 1–22.

Muniz Jr, J., Wintersberger, D., & Hong, J. L. (2022). Worker and manager judgments about factors that facilitate knowledge-sharing: Insights from a Brazilian automotive assembly line. *Knowledge and Process Management*, *29*(2), 132–146.

Nakano, D. (2006). Reframing Knowledge Management: a study of perspectives and related processes. In *2nd. European Conference on Management of Technology Proceedings*. Birmingham: Proceedings.

Nakano, D., Muniz, J., Jr., & Batista, E. D., Jr. (2013). Engaging environments: Tacit knowledge sharing on the shop floor. *Journal of Knowledge Management*, *17*(2), 290–306.

Nakash, M., & Bouhnik, D. (2021). Knowledge management is not dead. It has changed its appearance. And it will continue to change. *Knowledge and Process Management*, *28*(1), 29–39.

Nascimento, L. O., Muniz, J., Jr., & Wintersberger, D. (2022). *Skills for Industry 4.0 preparedness: The case of workers within Brazilian Automotive Assembly Lines* (working paper).

Núñez-Merino, M., Maqueira-Marín, J. M., Moyano-Fuentes, J., & Martínez-Jurado, P. J. (2020). Information and digital technologies of Industry 4.0 and Lean supply chain management: A systematic literature review. *International Journal of Production Research*, *58*(16), 5034–5061.

OECD. (2017). *The next production revolution: Implications for governments and business*. Organisation for Economic Co-operation and Development OECD. https://www.oecd.org/innovation/the-next-production-revolution-9789264271036-en.htm

OICA. (2021). *Production statistics*. Organisation Internationale des Constructeurs d'Automobiles. https://www.oica.net/wp-content/uploads/By-country-region-2020.pdf

Peters, C., Maglio, P., Badinelli, R., Harmon, R. R., Maull, R., Spohrer, J. C., & Moghaddam, Y. (2016). Emerging digital frontiers for service innovation. *Communications of the Association for Information Systems: CAIS*, *1*(39), online.

Prinz, C., Morlock, F., Freith, S., Kreggenfeld, N., Kreimeier, D., & Kuhlenkötter, B. (2016). Learning factory modules for smart factories in industrie 4.0. *Procedia CiRp*, *54*, 113–118.

Radziwon, A., Bilberg, A., Bogers, M., & Madsen, E. S. (2014). The smart factory: Exploring adaptive and flexible manufacturing solutions. *Procedia Engineering*, *69*, 1184–1190.

Ribeiro, V. B., Nakano, D. N., & Muniz, J., Jr. (2022). *Knowledge management and Industry 4.0: A critical analysis and future agenda* (working paper).

Schneider, P. (2018). Managerial challenges of Industry 4.0: An empirically backed research agenda for a nascent field. *Review of Managerial Science*, *12*(3), 803–848.

Shamim, S., Cang, S., Yu, H., & Li, Y. (2016, July). *Management approaches for Industry 4.0: A human resource management perspective*. In *2016 IEEE Congress on Evolutionary Computation (CEC)* (pp. 5309–5316).

Sié, L., & Yakhlef, A. (2009). Passion and expertise knowledge transfer. *Journal of Knowledge Management*, *13*(4), 175–186.

Sony, M., & Naik, S. (2020). Industry 4.0 integration with socio-technical systems theory: A systematic review and proposed theoretical model. *Technology in Society*, *61*, 101248.

Szász, L., Demeter, K., Rácz, B. G., & Losonci, D. (2020). Industry 4.0: A review and analysis of contingency and performance effects. *Journal of Manufacturing Technology Management*, *32*(3), 667–694.

Thomas, N. (2020). Debates around the nature of knowledge transfer: How well do we know about the construct? *VINE Journal of Information and Knowledge Management Systems*, *50*(3), 409–425.

Thomas, A. J., Barton, R., & John, E. G. (2008). Advanced manufacturing technology implementation: A review of benefits and a model for change. *International Journal of Productivity and Performance Management*, *57*(2), 156–176.

Tohidinia, Z., & Mosakhani, M. (2010). Knowledge sharing behaviour and its predictors. *Industrial Management & Data Systems*, *110*(4), 611–631.

Uhlemann, T. H. J., Schock, C., Lehmann, C., Freiberger, S., & Steinhilper, R. (2017). The digital twin: Demonstrating the potential of real time data acquisition in production systems. *Procedia Manufacturing*, *9*, 113–120.

Wang, S., & Noe, R. A. (2010). Knowledge sharing: A review and directions for future research. *Human Resource Management Review*, *20*, 115–131.

Williamson, P., & Zeng, M. (2009). *Chinese Multinationals: Emerging through new global gateways*. In R. Ramamurti, & J. Singh (Eds.), *Emerging multinationals in emerging markets 81–109*. Cambridge University Press.

Wollschlaeger, M., Sauter, T., & Jasperneite, J. (2017). The future of industrial communication: Automation networks in the era of the internet of things and Industry 4.0. *IEEE Industrial Electronics Magazine*, *11*(1), 17–27.

Xu, L. D., Xu, E. L., & Li, L. (2018). Industry 4.0: State of the art and future trends. *International Journal of Production Research*, *56*(8), 2941–2962.

Yang, F., & Gu, S. (2021). Industry 4.0, a revolution that requires technology and national strategies. *Complex & Intelligent Systems*, *7*(3), 1311–1325.

Zezulka, F., Marcon, P., Vesely, I., & Sajdl, O. (2016). Industry 4.0–An introduction in the phenomenon. *IFAC-PapersOnLine*, *49*(25), 8–12.

Appendices

Appendix I

Interview Guide

A semi-structured interview guide (Costilhas, 2020) was developed for interviewing managers with experience working with blue-collar workers in both countries (Table A1) in order to understand their perception about cultural differences between the Brazilian and Chinese on the shop floor:

1. What are the characteristics of Brazilian and Chinese workers?
2. What is the difference between Brazilian and Chinese workers?
3. How does the Brazilian manager deal with Brazilian workers?
4. How does the Chinese manager deal with Chinese workers?
5. What's the incentive approach to Brazilian workers?
6. What's the incentive approach to Chinese workers?
7. What's the punishing approach to Brazilian workers?
8. What's the punishing approach to Chinese workers?
9. How is the Union influence over the Brazilian worker?
10. How is the Union influence over the Chinese worker?
11. What are the personal values of the Brazilian workers?
12. What are the personal values of the Chinese workers?
13. What are the organization systems in Chinese companies?
14. What are the organization systems in Brazilian companies?
15. How does the Chinese worker work/deal with other workers?
16. How does the Brazilian worker work/deal with other workers?
17. What were the difficulties encountered when you were working with the Chinese/Brazilian?
18. How did you overcome them? Any examples?
19. What are the similarities between Brazilian and Chinese workers?
20. Why do you think such problems/difficulties occur?
21. What are the similarities between Brazilian and Chinese workers?

22 How do the Brazilian workers share knowledge and experience in the industrial environment?
23 How do the Chinese workers share knowledge and experience in the industrial environment?
24 What's the concern about sharing knowledge in the Brazilian companies?
25 What's the concern about sharing knowledge in the Chinese companies?

The interviews were individually conducted in a one-hour virtual meeting with each manager (Table A1), which were recorded and transcribed.

Content analysis technique (Stemler, 2000) was applied to identify conceptual categories and the cultural aspects related to the production context in both countries (Table A2). The illustrative example below demonstrated how the content analysis was conducted among the meaning unit originated from interview, condensed meaning units and codes (i.e., Manager indicates the fragment answer (condensed meaning unit) 'afraid of losing his/her job' was translated to the factor (code) job security).

Table A1 Managers interviewed

Job function (CODE)	*Business*	*Professional experience (years)*	*China experience (years)*	*Brazil experience (years)*	*Nationality*
Advanced Manufacture Engineering Manager (MANENGEL)	Energy	20	6	14	Brazilian
Operation Director (DIROPAUT)	Automotive	30	5	25	Brazilian
Process Developing Supervisor (SUPAUT)	Automotive	20	1	19	Brazilian
Acquisition Director (DIRAQAUT)	Automotive	22	3	19	Brazilian
Commercial Manager (MANCOMEL1)	Energy infrastructure	8	4	4	Chinese
Commercial Manager (MAGCOMEL2)	Energy infrastructure	7	2	5	Chinese
Manager Engineering Toyota (MANENGTOY)	Automotive	20	0	20	Brazilian
Manager Production Toyota (MANPRODTOY)	Automotive	19	0	15	Brazilian

Table A2 Example of content analysis

Meaning unit	*Condensed meaning unit*	*Codes*
The Brazilian manager has less strength of authority and more commitment than the Chinese; in other words, in China, the hierarchy is very strong and important, sometimes the boss is a military man. The hierarchy of the Chinese company is like an army; the Chinese bosses don't even talk to the factory floor workers; however, he treats all employees equally, without personal colleagues and always respecting the hierarchy. The Brazilian bosses usually have a commitment and a strong relationship with everyone around him. In Brazil, the motivation is based on inspiring the workers to feel proud to belong in that organization; the company make this happen through a bunch of programmes like programme of veterans, improvement programmes, awards, programme of breaking barriers etc. They even offer dinners and coffee with directors and superiors, all to make them to feel part of the team. Often this relationship and programmes are more motivational than the salary itself. (DIROPAUT)	In China, the *hierarchy* is very strong and important, sometimes the *boss is a military man. The hierarchy of the Chinese company is like an army*; the Chinese bosses don't even talk to the factory floor workers.	Authority
In Brazil, when the employee does something stupid [wrong], he ends up being fired, there [China] you do not see much of it, the Chinese end up changing the employee of area trying to get it right; in other words, there are employees who have already expired and yet are in the company. Brazilian likes recognition does not need promotion, but a recognition of the boss, while the Chinese wants a financial pleasure and recognition in public, he wants people around to see the boss happy with his work. (MANENGEL)	Brazilian likes recognition *does not need promotion* but a *recognition of the boss*, while the Chinese wants a financial pleasure and *recognition* in public, he [Chinese] wants people around to *see the boss happy with his work.*	Performance orientation *Guanxi* Face *Guanxi*
The Brazilian worker is afraid of losing his/her job, while the Chinese comes from a communist policy, where companies are more preventive, the chance of him/her losing his/her job would be smaller, but today there are many companies that do not belong to the government. (MANENGEL)	The Brazilian worker is *afraid of losing his/her job*	Job security

(*Continued*)

Table A2 Example of content analysis (*Continued*)

Meaning unit	*Condensed meaning unit*	*Codes*
It was not possible to talk to the operators and supervisors, they did not speak English. It was necessary to take a manager to translate for us. In administrative area, everybody spoke English. It was very easy to make them follow the rules, and the procedures. They were not very disciplined but also not reactive to follow the procedures. They never said no. Sometimes they did not do something because were not able to do. But it is easy to work with them, they are friendly. The biggest problem was the language. Most of the time we needed someone to speak Chinese so that we could communicate. For example, if we need to rework a tool, it was necessary to wait for someone, to explain it in English and this person could explain in Chinese. It took a lot of time to make any tooling or maintenance modification or implementation and it was very difficult to explain it to Brazilian leadership team. (SUPAUT)	*They never said no. Sometimes they did not do something because were not able to do.*	Transparency
What happens is that China has been experiencing economic growth for a long time, so China is in a position to full employment chances, which makes the company the showcase of the employee, who can change it at any time. (MANENGEL)	Economic growth	Performance orientation

Appendix II

Questionnaire

Welcome

Our university is conducting research in industry. You have been invited to answer this questionnaire because of your experience and/or leadership in the shop floor processes. The objective of the research is to evaluate the factors that in your opinion contribute to better knowledge sharing among workers. We need your cooperation in answering this questionnaire. Certainly, you will answer it in about 20 minutes and this effort will be very useful to better know the shop floor and guide improvement opportunities in plants. Feel free to answer what you think, because the questions are simple and do not involve confidential aspects of where you work. The profile data is confidential.

Note the example below to help in your responses.

Example: For a football team to get victory in a match, check the degree of importance for a better alternative.

Importance of intensity	*Definition (... an alternative to the other)*
1	Equal importance
3	Moderate importance
5	Strong importance
7	Very strong
9	Extreme importance

A	Players individual skills	9	7	5	**3**	1	3	5	7	9	Integration among the players
B	Integration among the players	9	7	5	3	1	3	5	**7**	9	Number of fans in a match

A. This answer indicates that the individual skill of the players was considered to have little importance (3) compared to the integration among the players.

B. This answer indicates that the number of fans in a game (7) was considered to have great importance compared to integration between the players.

From now on, your judgement will be based on alternatives known as training, job instruction, 5S and others. Here are some definitions to avoid doubts. Now use the same scale and check the degree of importance of the following alternatives:

- Resources: Roles and responsibilities of HR, materials and resources time;
- Communication: Exchange of information, ideas and feeling;
- Incentives: Reward or recognition.

TO ANSWER PLEASE KEEP IN MIND THE OBJECTIVE OF BETTER SHARING KNOWLEDGE AMONG WORKERS

To ensure improved knowledge sharing between workers, based on the scale, check the relative significance of the following alternatives:

Conversation among plant workers	9	7	5	3	1	3	5	7	9	Registering at the standard operating procedure
Registering at the standard operating procedure	9	7	5	3	1	3	5	7	9	Studying the standard operating procedure

To ensure improved conversation among plant workers, check the degree of relative importance of the following alternative:

Objective	9	7	5	3	1	3	5	7	9	Structure
Structure	9	7	5	3	1	3	5	7	9	Communication
Communication	9	7	5	3	1	3	5	7	9	Training
Training	9	7	5	3	1	3	5	7	9	Personal characteristics
Personal characteristics	9	7	5	3	1	3	5	7	9	Personal relationship
Personal relationship	9	7	5	3	1	3	5	7	9	Problem-solving methodology
Problem-solving methodology	9	7	5	3	1	3	5	7	9	Standard operating procedure
Standard operating procedure	9	7	5	3	1	3	5	7	9	5S
5S	9	7	5	3	1	3	5	7	9	Poka-yoke
Poka-yoke	9	7	5	3	1	3	5	7	9	Quick changeover
Quick changeover	9	7	5	3	1	3	5	7	9	Incentive

To ensure improved registration in standard operating procedure, check the degree of relative importance to the following alternative:

Objective	9	7	5	3	1	3	5	7	9	Structure
Structure	9	7	5	3	1	3	5	7	9	Communication
Communication	9	7	5	3	1	3	5	7	9	Training
Training	9	7	5	3	1	3	5	7	9	Personal characteristics
Personal characteristics	9	7	5	3	1	3	5	7	9	Personal relationship
Personal relationship	9	7	5	3	1	3	5	7	9	Problem-solving methodology
Problem-solving methodology	9	7	5	3	1	3	5	7	9	Standard operating procedure
Standard operating procedure	9	7	5	3	1	3	5	7	9	5S
5S	9	7	5	3	1	3	5	7	9	Poka-yoke
Poka-yoke	9	7	5	3	1	3	5	7	9	Quick changeover
Quick changeover	9	7	5	3	1	3	5	7	9	Incentive

To ensure improved understanding of the standard operating procedure, check the degree of relative importance of the following alternative:

Objective	9	7	5	3	1	3	5	7	9	Structure
Structure	9	7	5	3	1	3	5	7	9	Communication
Communication	9	7	5	3	1	3	5	7	9	Training
Training	9	7	5	3	1	3	5	7	9	Personal characteristics
Personal characteristics	9	7	5	3	1	3	5	7	9	Personal relationship
Personal relationship	9	7	5	3	1	3	5	7	9	Problem-solving methodology
Problem-solving methodology	9	7	5	3	1	3	5	7	9	Standard operating procedure
Standard operating procedure	9	7	5	3	1	3	5	7	9	5S
5S	9	7	5	3	1	3	5	7	9	Poka-yoke
Poka-yoke	9	7	5	3	1	3	5	7	9	Quick changeover
Quick changeover	9	7	5	3	1	3	5	7	9	Incentive

RESPONDENT'S PROFILE (who works or has worked directly with workers)

Time of Industry Experience [years]: _____ Time as executive [years]: ______

Do you work directly in the production area? Yes ( ) No ( )

If "Yes" was your answer, in which area are you working? __________________

Your current position: ________________________

If "No" was your answer, have you ever worked in the production area? Yes ( ) No ( )

Was it easy to understand the questions? Yes ( ) No ( )

If "No" was your answer, tell us what you think was hard to understand: ______

____

Notes and/or comments: ____

Appendix III

Industry 4.0 in Brazil and China

The new manufacturing approach is known variously as Industry 4.0 (I4.0) in Germany (EU Parliament 2016; GTAI, 2019; Helmrich, 2015) and Brazil (MCTI, 2019), and under the strategic concept of 'Made in China 2025', also known as the 'Chinese version of Industry 4.0' that has been promoted by the Chinese government since 2015.

Countries, such as Germany, Canada, China and the United States, have been developing their advanced technology. Their governments have implemented long-term strategies as well as fostering short-term actions towards I4.0, which is a global phenomenon with a strong impact on their national economies. However, there is a concern for the local employment and the qualifications needed from workers for the implementation of I4.0 in different countries (Muniz et al., in press). Arbix et al. (2017) compared similar programmes implemented in Germany, the United States and China, and the authors highlight the following concerns:

1 These programmes work with focus, priorities and high volume of resources;
2 They pave the way for emerging industries;
3 They increase public-private dialogue and collaboration;

4 They generate new venture capital funds and support for technology start-ups;
5 They promote the internationalization of companies and institutions of science, technology and innovation;
6 They establish more innovation-friendly regulatory frameworks;
7 They make intensive use of public procurement systems;
8 They support projects with high economic, technological and social impact;
9 They make governance systems more efficient and transparent;
10 They seek cleaner and more sustainable production.

The government has an important role in the formulation of public policies by ensuring that different sectors in the economy can absorb and develop new technologies and are aligned with national and international trade regulations (Muniz et al., in press). This Appendix discusses Brazilian and Chinese public actions related to the implementation of I4.0.

Industry 4.0 in Brazil

Dalenogare et al. (2018) mention potential difficulties associated with the implementation of new technologies in emerging economies. Several challenges must be tackled to make I4.0 a reality in Brazil related to information technology infrastructure (i.e., 5G), energy efficiency, complexity of manufacturing systems, policies, legislation, concerns regarding the access to and use of personal data, organizational culture, employment and qualification of workers, which force the country to import technology from other countries, such as China.

According to the Brazilian Confederation of Industry (CNI, 2018, p. 19), the country has been successively losing positions in the global competitiveness ranking of the World Economic Forum. Brazil reached the worst position in the last ten years in 2017. The loss of national competitiveness compromises economic growth and the generation of jobs and income. According to the Inter-Union Department of Statistics and Socio-Economic Studies (DIEESE, 2021), Brazil took the opposite direction to that of other countries, such as Germany, the United States and China, deactivating or weakening industrial policy marks, which reduced industry influence in the GDP.

In order to establish policies aimed at l4.0, the Institute for Studies in Industrial Development – IEDI (2017) suggests nine (nine) strategic actions: (1) to bind public financing programmes for the purchase of machinery or access to working capital credit programmes; (2) to adopt similar action, but aimed at relevant sector clusters; (3) to develop more advanced technologies and production methods, but which are still unknown by most Brazilian industrial companies; (4) to constitute prototypes of production units with high levels of automation and funding shared among interested organizations and companies; (5) to prepare professionals focused on the main technologies of I4.0.; (6) to support advanced scientific skills training programmes for I4.0; (7) to attract highly trained human resources; (8) to develop human resources articulated to the formation of appropriate technological bases for the construction and dissemination of solutions; and (9) to acquire companies holding I4.0 structuring technologies.

The Brazilian Ministry of Science, Technology and Innovation (MCTI) published the 'Action Plan for the Brazilian Chamber of Industry 4.0 in Brazil: 2019-2022', which aims to induce the use of concepts and practices related to I4.0. The plan highlights some concerns, including (1) increasing competitiveness and productivity of Brazilian companies through I4.0; (2) introducing the use of I4.0 technologies in small- and medium-sized companies; (3) guaranteeing appropriate instruments so that technology-based company solutions can be offered and made available directly to companies; (4) ensuring stability and volume of resources at an affordable cost for the implementation of initiatives aimed at I4.0; and (5) avoiding overlapping efforts by public and private institutions to solve the needs and demands of I4.0 in the country (MCTI, 2019).

Likewise, the MCTI (2019) established some actions related to the regulatory mark of I4.0: (1) promote the establishment and dissemination of technical regulations and standards related to I4.0.; (2) encourage the provision of appropriate infrastructure and technological environments to support I4.0; and (3) promote the use of financial instruments to allow small suppliers to obtain financing for the construction of access networks. The Action Plan lists actions and initiatives to overcome the concerns related to the implementation of I4.0 in Brazil:

- Increase the competitiveness and productivity of Brazilian companies through I4.0;
- Improve Brazil's insertion in global value chains;
- Introduce the use of I4.0 technologies in small- and medium-sized companies;
- Ensure solutions from technology-based companies, start-ups and integrators can be offered and made available directly to companies;
- Ensure stability and volume of resources at an adequate cost to implement initiatives for I4.0;
- Identify and develop solutions for I4.0 suitable for companies in the Brazilian production sector;
- Avoid overlapping individual efforts by public and private institutions to solve the needs and demands of I4.0 in Brazil.

The Brazilian Action Plan (MCTI, 2019) foresees public and private efforts aimed at executing actions and initiatives related to the following themes:

- Technological development and innovation: To promote innovation and development of enabling technologies and Industry 4.0 solutions by Brazilian companies;
- Human capital: To have qualified human resources to work in the environment of Economy 4.0 and in the development of related technologies;

- Production chains and supplier development: To promote the adoption of enabling technologies and solutions for Industry 4.0 in companies of all sizes with a view to increasing productivity;
- Regulation, technical standardization and infrastructure: To create and/or improve standardization and regulation instruments and develop infrastructure aimed at improving the environment for the development of Industry 4.0 in Brazil.

Regarding the regulatory mark, it is necessary to implement lines of support aimed at updating manufacturing plants, technological infrastructure and training of employees; and, secondly, to provide the necessary conditions to allow the participation of different industrial segments in the elaboration of technical standards that regulate the technological activities developed under I4.0.

IndustriAll Global Union (2017) highlights that I4.0 creates opportunities for different workers, as long as they have access to (re)education, (re)qualification and specialized training. A labour context with a reduction in wages, job insecurity, reduction of employment and competition between human productivity versus machines needs to be mitigated. Socio-economic aspects such as the lack of qualified labour and the postponement of retirement due to the ageing of society affect the implementation of I4.0 (Peruzzini & Pellicciari, 2017; Shamim et al., 2016).

The MCTI reveals some human resource challenges and the Brazilian plans to have qualified human resources to work in the context of I4.0 technologies through three major actions related to (1) promote training and re-qualification of teachers in skills and abilities for the 4.0 economy; (2) promote the qualification, development and retraining of professionals for the 4.0 economy; and (3) develop educational skills and competences for the 4.0 economy.

The new Brazilian Curricular Guidelines for the Engineering Undergraduate Course are a recent achievement of the governmental, industrial and academic sectors (Masetto et al., 2010). The new guidelines seem to solve formative's problems, while pointing to other demands arising from the current reality, which requires the formation of more and better engineers through, among other actions, the development of soft skills (Aravena-Reyes, 2021). From the guidelines, Brazilian engineering universities are reviewing their curriculums from 2022 to provide content and practices to prepare future engineers to the I4.0 market. In addition, industries need to provide complementary conditions to (re)qualify and/or encourage their workers' continued education towards the development of skills and competences in line with the new technological context.

Among the challenges mentioned by the CNI (2018), education is referred to at three levels: basic, professional and higher education. They understand that the increase in productivity and competitiveness depends on the quality of education, that is, the professional training of the worker. They also highlight the unsatisfactory quality of basic education and the reduced offer of technical and professional training are barriers to productivity growth and company competitiveness. Despite its islands of excellence, higher education in Brazil is far from fulfilling the demands of the productive sector and the best world references for quality, which places the country at a disadvantageous position in terms of its ability to innovate and compete (CNI, 2018, p. 76).

The alignment between academic training and industry needs to challenge the university in several areas, especially in Production Engineering. The Brazilian education system has 805 undergraduate courses in Production Engineering (INEP, 2017) and 49 graduate courses in Production Engineering (CAPES, 2020).

The Brazilian Association of Industrial Research and Innovation (EMBRAPII), a social organization qualified by the Federal Government in operation since 2013, whose mission is to 'Contribute to the development of innovation and competitiveness of industry in Brazil' (EMBRAPII, n.d., p.7), has 42 accredited units that work with agility, flexibility and reduced risk when it comes to supporting Research, Development and Innovation (RD&I) projects by Brazilian companies. According to EMBRAPII (n.d.), the non-reimbursable resources are applied to projects that present a technological focus and capacity to meet the companies' RD&I demands.

In its 2017–2019 Master Plan, EMBRAPII established six strategic guidelines: (1) develop financing mechanisms; (2) participate in the industry's innovation strategy map; (3) define strategic areas for public calls; (4) strengthen the EMBRAPII brand among its main stakeholders; (5) develop the network of EMBRAPII Units; and (6) develop structuring actions for EMBRAPII (headquarters) (EMBRAPII, n.d.).

The 2030 Agenda for Sustainable Development, adopted by all United Nations Member States in 2015, provides a shared blueprint for peace and prosperity for people and the planet, now and into the future (UN, 2022). At its heart are the 17 Sustainable Development Goals (SDGs), which are an urgent call for action by all countries – developed and developing – in a global partnership. They recognize that ending poverty and other deprivations must go hand-in-hand with strategies that improve health and education, reduce inequality and spur economic growth – all while tackling climate change and working to preserve our oceans and forests.

De-industrialization, pandemic and the political scenario in Brazil have enhanced the crisis in the economy, industrial competitiveness and employment. This scenario has impacted the implementation of I4.0 in Brazil, whose context is different from the aforementioned countries. Brazilian government actions indicate an agenda to implement I4.0 aligned with the Sustainable Development Goals (Muniz et al., in press), through work and economic growth (SDG-8), construction of infrastructure to promote industrialization and innovation (SDG-9), new educational methods (SDG-4) and global partnership for sustainable development (SDG-17), which collide with the reality of decreasing of competitiveness (CNI, 2018), an industrial park that has little maturity for the I4.0 (SENAI, 2019), closing of plants such as Ford's, indicating a potential process of de-industrialization and unemployment (Lima & Dulci, 2021) and the political-economic crisis resulting in reduced investments in science and technology, and public universities (USP, 2022). However, initiatives led by the private organizations themselves are identified.

Industry 4.0 in China

China has accumulated rich experience in implementing nationwide strategic plans. In order to prevent China's economy from collapse and lift hundreds of millions of people out of poverty, China's paramount leader Deng Xiaoping initiated a programme of economic reform in its open door policy to foreign investors in 1978 when the country found itself in a period of political uncertainty and operating a rigid centrally planned economic system (Li, 2013). Its economic reform started with a pilot city in Shenzhen and established the special economic zone (SEZ) (Li, 2018). The special economic zone experimented with free market business models paired with a state planning policy, providing subsidiary and preferential tax benefits to foreign firms that were interested in and doing business in China (China in Brief, 2012). During this incubation period, manufacturing companies experimented with a Chinese-style approach to foreign investment and to the development of an export-based manufacturing focus for China to open up to the international market (Li, 2013).

The demarcation between the navigation period and the incubation period was the establishment of Shanghai Pudong New Zone in 1992. The objective of this New Zone was to evolve from the production of low-cost, low-technology content products to high-tech-oriented products by attracting global investment (Li, 2005). The Chinese government extended the reforms from the establishment of SEZ to the creation of a socialist market economy (Zhu, 2011). Some important measures included refining central economic control, tightening fiscal and monetary policies and managing the scale of fixed-assets investment, which the Chinese government took in the navigation years (Li, 2013).

With China's joining in the WTO in 2001, many US and European firms moved their manufacturing operations into China, either through outsourcing or joint ventures (Li, 2013). Meanwhile, China's economic reforms created a versatile manufacturing infrastructure that provided fertile soil for the global manufacturing supply chain to grow (Li, 2013). The strategic turn made by the developed nations in the late 1990s provided a fertile ground for the poise of the Made-in-China paradigm (Li, 2013). However, the investment in and development of manufacturing processing infrastructure alone was not enough, because people who operate manufacturing systems need to be educated and equipped with the capability and skills to run the system (Li, 2013). Thus, revitalization through education was a critical attribute of the growth in the dynamic years (Li, 2013). Education can be a leading soft power trait that will impact a nation's economic success and manufacturing capability (Li, 2013). Thus, Li (2013) concluded that a low-cost and educated workforce paired with top-notch innovation and engineering capacity could help China build core competitiveness in the dynamic period.

After years of economic development, China's manufacturing growth has entered a new era (Li, 2018). Resources and environmental constraints continue to intensify, labour and material costs keep on increasing, environmental responsibility continues to increase, foreign direct investment flows and export growth have slowed down (Li, 2018). Rethinking its model of economic development based on manufacturing is thus imperative in response to the recent global re-industrialization tide and Germany's high-tech strategy 'Industry 4.0'; in 2015, China's State Council released a ten-year strategic development plan for the Chinese manufacturing industry, called Made in China 2025 (MIC2025) (China's State Council, 2015). MIC2025 is the first step to transform China into a world-leading manufacturing power and was regarded as the Chinese version of I4.0 (Wang et al., 2020).

The purpose of MIC2025 is to promote technology breakthroughs in ten key sectors: new information technology, numerical control tools and robotics, aerospace equipment, ocean engineering equipment and high-tech ships, railway equipment, energy saving and new energy vehicles (NEVs), power equipment, new materials, biological medicine and medical devices and agricultural machinery (China's State Council, 2015). Between 2000 and 2016, China's Gross Expenditure on R&D measured in current PPP$ has been increasing by approximately 18% annually (Ministry of Science and Technology, various years). In 2019, Gross Domestic Spending on R&D in China came close to that of the United States, reaching $514.8 billion and ranking the second place in G7 countries (OECD, 2022).

According to Li (2018), GDP, FDI net flows and high technology exports are key elements of manufacturing capability to implement MIC2025 successfully. China's GDP has been increasing continuously from US$11.06 trillion to US$14.72 trillion from 2015 to 2020 (World Bank, 2020a–c). The FDI net inflows and high technology exports have started to decrease in 2013 and remain steady since 2017 (The World Bank, 2020a–2020c). From 2012 to 2021, the added value of manufacturing industry has increased from 16.98 trillion yuan to 31.4 trillion yuan and has ranked first in the world for 12 consecutive years (China's State Council, 2022). The data indicates that China has become more reliant on its own investment and domestic consumption of high-tech products.

By 2021, China has built 21 national manufacturing innovation centres, 2 national and local manufacturing innovation centres, and 223 provincial level manufacturing innovation centres (China's State Council, 2022). In 2021, the competitive advantages of photovoltaic, wind power, shipbuilding and other industrial chains will be further enhanced (China's State Council, 2022). Progress has been made in tackling key problems in new displays, industrial machines and new materials (China's State Council, 2022). Moreover, the growth rate of high-tech manufacturing industry and equipment manufacturing industry is significantly faster than that of the manufacturing industry, and the contribution rate to the growth of the above-scale industries has increased from 11.8% and 31.8% in 2015 to 28.6% and 45% in 2021, respectively (China's State Council, 2022). The digital, networked and intelligent transformation of the manufacturing industry has been further advanced. By 2021, the numerical control rate of key processes and the penetration rate of digital R&D design tools in industries nationwide reached 55.3% and 74.7%, respectively, with an increase of 30.7% and 25.9% compared to 2012 (China State Council, 2022).

Based on MIC2025, China has launched a strategy called Internet Plus, which is to drive economic growth through the integration of Internet technologies with manufacturing and business (Al-Sayed & Yang, 2020). This includes integrating the mobile Internet, cloud computing, big data and Internet of Things (IoT) with modern manufacturing, fostering new industries and business development, in addition to e-commerce, industrial Internet and Internet finance (LehmanBrown, 2017). Government offered generous grants to promote IoT research and development, including offering preferential tax policies for the software and circuits industries (Al-Sayed & Yang, 2020). The market size of Chinese IoT has been rising from 742 billion yuan in 2015 to 1667 billion yuan in 2020 (Statistia, 2022).

The development of a sustainable auto industry is critical for building a low-carbon society, and the status of NEVs has advanced considerably in China recently (Wu et al., 2021). In 2020, the sales volume of NEVs reached 1.367 million, accounting for 40.7% of the world's total sales (Wu et al., 2021).

Since 2010, China's new energy industry has developed rapidly, and this development trend is marginally increasing (Pan & Dong, 2022). China's cumulative installed photovoltaic generation capacity reached approximately 50.61 GW (Zhang & Zhang, 2020) by 2018 and had the world's largest installed wind turbine capacity, accounting for 35.7% of the world's volume (Zhang et al., 2020).

The global competition now is no longer in the area of low-cost labour production, but in a stage of Internet-Plus Manufacturing that competes for talent, human capital and intellectual property (Li, 2013). Three types of talents have been planned to be developed in MIC2025, including skilled labour workforce, professional, technical and management talents and innovation and entrepreneurship talents (Al-Sayed & Yang, 2020). Educational institutions have cultivated hundreds and thousands of university graduates that can contribute to the economic growth. The number of graduates from public collage and universities in China is increasing steadily from 6,809,000 in 2015 to 7,972,000 in 2020 (China Statistical Yearbook 2021). In the past 10 years, there are more and more Chinese students returning from abroad. By 2019, there are 580,300 returned study-abroad students, which increases about 437% in the period 2009–2019 (China Statistical Yearbook, 2021). Li (2018) stated that these highly educated with global vision have benefited China in the past 30 years.

Based on the statistics shown above, according to Li (2018), young people in China will not willing to take low-cost blue-collar jobs in the next ten years since MIC2025 values high-tech professional career. The urbanization rate has increased steadily in China over the last decades, and 64.7% of the total population in China is living in cities in 2021 (National Bureau of Statistics of China, 2022). Urban residents have now exceeded the rural residents, and one associated phenomenon is the migration of working people from rural to urban areas, which before was highly restricted but now is common (Li et al., 2018). This migration reduces the supply of low-cost labour since the rural population is the major source of low-cost labour (Li, 2018). Nevertheless, China is becoming less competitive in the traditional manufacturing sector relative to certain emerging economies, such as India, Indonesia and Vietnam since it no longer relies heavily on labour-intensive and low-cost manufacturing exports (Cui et al., 2018). The mismatching problems in China's labour market occur since low-skilled workers are the majority of China's migrant labour (Cui et al., 2018). Against the background of the ongoing structural transformation and industrial upgrading, the shortage of high-skilled workers is increasing, which implies the challenge of transforming labour markets featuring traditional industries to those for emerging industries (Li et al., 2022).

Moreover, that HRM as context-specific management practice is now well understood and agreed upon (Mayrhofer et al., 2019). Changes in geopolitical landscape, such as rising nationalism and protectionism under MIC2025, have dampened China's expanding role in the global economy and increased the political and economic risks for Chinese companies operating at home and abroad (Cui et al., 2018). In order to protect China's economy from the Sino-US trade wars and national protectionism, the Chinese government launched the 'dual circulation' strategic plan in 2020 to reduce its dependence on overseas markets and technology in its long-term development (Yao, 2020). 'Internal circulation', that is, the domestic cycle of production, distribution and consumption, will now be the main economic model for China's future development, supported by innovation and upgrades in the economy (Yao, 2020).

The concept of 'dual circulation' forms part of China's 14th five-year plan (2021–2025) (Yao, 2020). The economic development of this period (2021–2025) is likely to be underpinned by innovation and technological upgrading, and the demand for innovative talents and high-skilled talents will further increase. How to develop, attract and retain talents has become a serious concern for the country, industry and companies (Cui et al., 2018). The problems of talent attraction and retention have been exacerbated by an unstable and uncertain political and economic environment. It creates a big challenge for an enterprise to maintain a sustainable competitive advantage by making good use of both domestic and foreign talent resources (Cui et al., 2018).

Final Consideration

Management challenges to support the implementation of I4.0, which includes training review, performance assessment, staff profile and organizational flexibility, are needed to overcome. Human resources programmes, including the implementation of new training strategies are necessary in order to prepare employees to use/apply new technologies. Several researchers have already addressed the technical and personal skills for workers to act in this new context, namely IT security, ability to work under pressure, creativity to solve problems, research and communication skills (Muniz et al., in press).

Universities and companies are responsible for the development of professionals. However, they work separately and independently in Brazil. Technological change poses challenges for teaching, especially in the fields of Engineering. The implementation of I4.0 demands an academic and business agenda to prepare the professionals, professors and learners who are able to work with these technologies and apply them to generate income and social well-being, highlighting the difficulties in implementing new technologies in emerging economies.

Important factors for the implementation of I4.0 belong to the domain of knowledge management and people management, which are concerned with managerial support and leadership, culture, information and communication technology, strategy and objective, measurement, organizational infrastructure, processes and activities, motivational incentives, training and personal characteristics. These challenges underpinned a new manufacturing trend that indicates a new relationship between technology and the workers.

References

Al-Sayed, R., & Yang, J. (2020). Towards Chinese smart manufacturing ecosystem in the context of the one belt one road initiative. *Journal of Science and Technology Policy Management*, *11*(3), 291–310.

Aravena-Reyes, J. (2021). Rumo a uma Formação Social do Engenheiro: Crítica às Novas Diretrizes Curriculares de Engenharia. (Portuguese). *Trabalho & Educação*, *30*(2), 141–158.

Arbix, G., Salerno, M. S., Zancul, E., Amaral, G., & Lins, L. M. (2017). O Brasil e a nova onda de manufatura avançada: o que aprender com Alemanha, China e Estados Unidos. (Portuguese). *Novos estudos CEBRAP*, *36*, 29–49.

CAPES. (2020). Coordenação de Aperfeiçoamento de Pessoal do Ensino Superior. Programas da Pós-Graduação Stricto Sensu no Brasil [2017-2020]. (Portuguese). https://dadosabertos.capes.gov.br/dataset. Acesso em: 22 out. 2021.

China in Brief. (2012). http://www.china.org.cn/e-china/openingup/sez.htm.

China Statistical Yearbook. (2021). http://www.stats.gov.cn/tjsj/ndsj/2021/indexeh.htm

CNI. (2018). Mapa estratégico da indústria 2018–2022. Brasília. (Portuguese) https://static.portaldaindustria.com.br/media/filer_public/ee/50/ee50ea49-2d62-42f6-a304-1972c32623d4/mapa_final_ajustado_leve_out_2018.pdf.

China State Council. (2015). Made in China 2025 Strategy (No.Guofa 2015–28). (Chinese).

China State Council. (2022). From Made in China to Created in China. (Chinese). http://www.gov.cn/xinwen/2022-03/21/content_5680150.htm.

Costilhas, A. A. M. (2020). Workers knowledge sharing improvements and the cultural influence: Comparative study Brazil and China in a capital good industry [Master's thesis]. School of Engineering of Guaratingueta, Sao Paulo State University, UNESP Repository. http://hdl.handle.net/11449/202394.

Cui, Y., Meng, J., & Lu, C. (2018). Recent developments in China's labor market: Labor shortage, rising wages and their implications. *Review of Development Economics*, *22*(3), 1217–1238.

Dalenogare, L. S., Benitez, G. B., Ayala, N. F., & Frank, A. G. (2018). The expected contribution of Industry 4.0 technologies for industrial performance. *International Journal of Production Economics*, *204*, 383–394.

DIEESE. (2021). A desindustrialização e o setor automotivo: retomada urgente ou crise sem fim. Nota Técnica. (Portuguese). https://www.dieese.org.br/notatecnica/2021/notaTec259desindustrializaSetorAutomotivo.pdf

EMBRAPII. (n.d.). Plano Diretor 2017–2019. https://embrapii.org.br/wp-content/images/2018/11/Plano-Diretor-EMBRAPII-2017-2019.pdf.

EU Parliament. (2016). Industry 4.0. Directorate General for Internal Policies, Policy Department A: Economic and Scientific Policy. Study for the ITRE committee. http://www.europarl.europa.eu/RegData/etudes/STUD/2016/570007/IPOL_STU(2016)570007_EN.pdf.

EXECUTIVE OFFICE OF THE US PRESIDENT. (2018). Strategy for American leadership in advanced manufacturing. National Science and Technology Council. https://trumpwhitehouse.archives.gov/wp-content/uploads/2018/10/Advanced-Manufacturing-Strategic-Plan-2018.pdf.

GTAI. (2019). Industrie 4.0. Germany Trade and Invest. https://www.gtai.de/GTAI/Navigation/EN/Invest/Industries/industrie-4-0.html.

Helmrich, K. (2015). On the way to industry 4.0-the digital enterprise. *Si*emens AG, Hannover Messe.

IEDI. (2017). Indústria 4.0: a quarta revolução industrial e os desafios para a indústria e para o desenvolvimento brasileiro. 50p. Disponível em: https://www.iedi.org.br/media/site/artigos/20170721_iedi_industria_4_0.pdf. Acesso em: 4 out. 2021.

IndustriALL Global Union. (2017). The challenge of industry 4.0 and the demand for new answers. http://www.industriall-union.org/sites/default/files/uploads/documents/2017/SWITZERLAND/Industry4point0Conf/draft_integrated_industry_4.0_paper_5_17.10.2017.pdf.

Instituto Nacional de Estudos e Pesquisas Educacionais Anísio Teixeira (INEP). (2017). Sinopse Estatística da Educação Superior 2017 (Portuguese). http://inep.gov.br/sinopses-estatisticas-da-educacao-superior.

Lima, R. J. D. C., & Dulci, J. A. (2021). Trabalhando sem A Ford: política industrial e ação corporativa em São Bernardo do Campo. *Revista Brasileira de Ciências Sociais*, *36*(107).

LehmanBrown. (2017). Made In China 2025 & Internet Plus: The 4th Industrial Revolution. Lehman Brown Insight https://www.lehmanbrown.com/news-and-events/made-china-2025-internet-plus-4th-industrial-revolution/.

Liao, Y., Deschamps, F., Loures, E. D. F. R., & Ramos, L. F. P. (2017). Past, present and future of Industry 4.0—A systematic literature review and research agenda proposal. *International Journal of Production Research*, *55*(12), 3609–3629.

Li, L. (2005). Assessing intermediate infrastructural manufacturing decisions that affect a firm's market performance. *International Journal of Production Research*, *43*(12), 2537–2551.

Li, L. (2013). The path to made-in-China: How this was done and future prospects. *International Journal of Production Economics*, *146*(1), 4–13.

Li, L. (2018). China's manufacturing locus in 2025: With a comparison of "Made-in-China 2025" and "Industry 4.0". *Technological Forecasting & Social Change*, *135*, 66–74.

Li, W., Sun, F., & Anderson, S. (2018). Differences in depressive symptoms between rural and urban Chinese labor force: The mediating effects of community factors. *International Journal of Social Psychiatry*, *64*(4), 317–325.

Li, Y., Wei, Y., Li, Y., Lei, Z., & Ceriani, A. (2022). Connecting emerging industry and regional innovation system: Linkages, effect and paradigm in China. *Technovation*, 111.

Masetto, M. T., Linhares, M. M. P., Keller-Franco, E., Gaeta, C., Zuzowky-Tavares, C., & Schulze, T. R. (2010). The cooperative curriculum in engineering: Curricular innovation and professors development. *Revista Profissão Docente*, *10*(22), 108–123.

Mayrhofer, W., Gooderham, P. N., & Brewster, C. (2019). Context and HRM: Theory, evidence, and proposals. *International Studies of Management & Organization*, *49*(4), 355–371.

Ministry of Science and Technology. (n.d). *China S&T statistical yearbook*. Ministry of Science and Technology.

Ministry of Industry and Information Technology of the People's Republic of China and Ministry of finance of the People's Republic of China. https://www.miit.gov.cn/.

Ministério da Ciência, Tecnologia, Inovações e Comunicações (MCTI, 2019). Plano de ação da Câmara Brasileira da Indústria 4.0 do Brasil: 2019-2022 (Portuguese). https://www.gov.br/economia/pt-br/centrais-de-conteudo/publicacoes/arquivos/camara_i40__plano_de_acaoversao_finalrevisada.pdf.

Muniz, J. Jr., Valentim, M. L. P., Wintersberger, D., Ramirez, P., & Zhang, Y. The relationship between Industry 4.0 with official Brazilian actions and the 2030 Agenda. In: Fernandes, B. M. (Org). *Building territories based on GDS leaving no one behind*. EDUNESP (in press).

National Bureau of Statistics of China. (2022). Stats. http://www.stats.gov.cn/tjsj/zxfb/202201/t20220117_1826404.html.

OECD. (2022). Gross Domestic Spending on R&D. OECD. https://data.oecd.org/rd/gross-domestic-spending-on-r-d.htm.

Pan, Y., & Dong, F. (2022). Dynamic evolution and driving factors of new energy development: Fresh evidence from China. *Technological Forecasting and Social Change*, *176*, 121475.

Peruzzini, M., & Pellicciari, M. (2017). A framework to design a human-centred adaptive manufacturing system for aging workers. *Advanced Engineering Informatics*, *33*, 330–349.

SENAI. (2019). SENAI avalia maturidade de empresas em Indústria 4.0 para indicar caminho de atualização tecnológica. https://www.senaigo.com.br/noticia-senai-avalia-maturidade-de-empresas-em-industria-40-para-indicar-caminho-de-atualizacao-tecnologica.

Shamim, S., Cang, S., Yu, H., & Li, Y. (2016, July). Management approaches for Industry 4.0: A human resource management perspective. In *2016 IEEE congress on evolutionary computation (CEC)* (pp. 5309–5316). IEEE.

Statistia. (2022). Market Size of Internet-of-Things (IoT) in China from 2009 to 2020 with an Estimate until 2025. https://www-statista-com.eu1.proxy.openathens.net/statistics/972077/china-internet-of-things-iot-market-size/.

Stemler, S. (2000). An overview of content analysis. *Practical Assessment, Research, and Evaluation*, *7*(1), 17.

United Nations (UN). (2022). https://sdgs.un.org/

USP. (2022). Orçamento federal para 2022 mantém ciência brasileira em situação de penúria (Portuguese). Federal budget for 2022 keeps Brazilian science in a situation of shortage. Jornal da USP. https://jornal.usp.br/atualidades/orcamento-2022-mantem-ciencia-brasileira-em-situacao-de-penuria/.

Wang, J., Wu, H., & Chen, Y. (2020). Made in China 2025 and manufacturing strategy decisions with reverse QFD. *International Journal of Production Economics*, *224*, 107539.

World Bank. (2020b). Foreign Direct Investment, Net Inflows (BoP, current US$) – China. https://data.worldbank.org/indicator/BX.KLT.DINV.CD.WD?locations=CN.

World Bank. (2020a). GDP (current US$) – China. https://data.worldbank.org/indicator/NY.GDP.MKTP.CD?locations=CN.

World Bank. (2020c). High-technology Exports (% of manufactured exports) – China. https://data.worldbank.org/indicator/TX.VAL.TECH.MF.ZS?end=2020&locations=CN&start=2007&view=chart.

Wu, Z., Shao, Q., Su, Y., & Zhang, D. (2021). A socio-technical transition path for new energy vehicles in China: A multi-level perspective. *Technological Forecasting and Social Change*, *172*, 121007.

Yao, K. (2020). What We Know About China's 'Dual Circulation' Economic Strategy. Reuters. https://www.reuters.com/article/china-economy-transformation-explainer-idUSKBN2600B5.

Zhu, R. (2011). Zhu Rongji meets the press. Oxford University Press. https://global.oup.com/academic/product/zhu-rongji-meets-the-press-9780193966413?cc=br&lang=en&

Zhang, M., & Zhang, Q. (2020). Grid parity analysis of distributed photovoltaic power generation in China. *Energy*, *206*, 118165.

Zhang, S., Wei, J., Chen, X., & Zhao, Y. (2020). China in global wind power development: Role, status and impact. *Renewable and Sustainable Energy Reviews*, *127*, 109881.

Index

Note: *Italicized* page numbers refer to figures, **bold** page numbers refer to tables, and page numbers with "n" refer to notes.

adaptability 105, 108
aggregating individual judgment (AIJ) method **87**, **95**, 102n1
aggregating individual priorities (AIP) method 102n2
Ahmed, T. 26
Alibaba 1
Ambev 1
Amin, A. 22
analytic hierarchy process (AHP) 17; data collection 83–86, **87**; methodology 82–86
Ardichvili, A. 43
Aristotle 21
assemblages of people 22
assembly: lines 77, 82, 98, 106–107, 110; procedures 81; workers 83
authority: GE Hydro 60–61; Maxion Wheels 67; power of 61; Toyota Motor Corporation 72–73
automotive industry 1, 9, 74, 109
autonomy 21, **23**, 29–30, 73, 89

Ba 96
Baena, F. 108
Bahamas 9
barriers: cross-cultural 15; knowledge sharing 26, 82, 105; organizational 25
Bhagat, R. 31–32, 45–46
Bisalyaputra, K. 21
blue-collar workers: challenges 108; Chinese 101; contextual knowledge and conventional wisdom 50; for digital transformation 110; incentives among 83; knowledge management in 29–31; knowledge sharing 15, 82–83; social interaction among 30
Brazil: Chinese enterprises investments 6; cultural values 47–52; economic development of 6–14; economic landscape in 10–11; financial recognition in 76; foreign direct investments (FDIs) *2*; GE Hydro Brazil 58, 82, 94; Industry 4.0 in 122–126; inward FDIs **8**, 8–10, **10**; knowledge sharing 47–52; Maxion Brazil 86; Maxion Wheels 66–71, 82; MNCs in 104; outward FDIs 6–8, *7*, **10**; socialization 89; Toyota Brazil 71; workers 77
Brazilian Industrial Confederation (CNI) 8, 122, 124
Brazilian society 48, 50
Brazilian way *(jeitinho Brasileiro)* 48–50, 63
BRICs 6, 11, 15–16, 41
British Petroleum (BP PLC) 9
Building Resilient Infrastructures (SDG-9) 107
Bureaucratic rules 49
Bureaucratization 49

case studies 58–79; GE Hydro 58–65; Maxion Wheels 66–71; Toyota Motor Corporation 71–78
China 1, 46; cultural values 41–47; economic development of 1–6; economic landscape in 10–11; economic reforms 126; foreign direct investments (FDIs) *2*; GDP 127; GE Hydro China 58, 82; Industry 4.0 in 126–129; internalization 102; Internet Plus 128; inward FDIs 3–5, **4**; knowledge sharing 41–47; labour market 129; manufacturing operations 126; Maxion Nantong

Wheels CO. Ltd 66, 86–94; MNCs in 104; outward FDIs 1–3, **2–3**; structure 93; Toyota China 71
Chinese-speaking countries 5–6
Choi, B. 25
collaboration **23**, 25, 30, 110
collective action 22
collective improvisation 22
collectivism 32, 44–46, 49, 70; horizontal 45–46; in-group 49; vertical 45–46
colonialism 48–49
communication **109**; affect on knowledge sharing 45; definition 29; face-to-face 51; formal 83; informal 29; interpersonal 47; and socialization 92; and tacit knowledge 22; verbal **23**; workers 50
competence 14, 42, 47, 124
competitiveness 126; global 122; industrial 20, 125; innovations 24; meritocracy 99, 100; national 122; of organizations 29
Complete Knock-Down (CKD) 71
complex decision making 83; *see also* decision-making
complexity 108, 122
conceptual foundation 24
conceptualization 20
conflicts: in Brazil and China 64, 70; between collective interests and self-interests 45; interpersonal 25, 30
Confucianism 67
context 124; in cross-cultural 31–33, 104, 111; *guanxi* 62; indigenous 48; knowledge management 26, 31–33; knowledge sharing 50–51, 84; production 15, 28, 104, 116; social and macroeconomic between Brazil and China 70; worker for I4.0 14
continuous improvement 20–21, 24–25, 49–50, 60, 74, 82, 92, 102, 111; tasks 29
countries: Asian 59, 72; BRICS 6, 11, 15–16; China and Portuguese-speaking 1, **5**, 5–6; with China's OFDIs **3**, 3–4; employment in Brazil and China 14; investing in Brazil 9; Latin American 58; with low trust culture 46–47; managers from developed 105; managers located in developing 105; manufacturing processes in China and Brazil 109; MNCs 15; power of authority in China and Brazil 61; production processes in China and Brazil 60; role of union in China and Brazil 77; South American 10
COVID-19 3–4, 9
craft/task knowing **23**
creativity 20, **23**, 48–49, 52, 93, 107, 129
cultural factors 32, 41, 104
cultural identity 49
cultural traits 48–49, 51–52
cultural values 16, 31–32, 41–52, 105; Chinese cultural values 41–47; collectivistic 44–45, 51; individualistic 45
culture 16–17, 20, 22, 25; American 99; Asian 67; Brazilian 50, 73, 76, 81; in China 44, 61, 64, 69–70, 81, 101; collectivist 33, 44–45, 47, 51; corporate 47; indigenous 17, 32, 105; individualistic 45; knowledge management friendly 49; knowledge sharing 26, 110; national 31–32, 41; organizational 41, 48, 122

Dalenogare, L. S. 108–109
data collection, analytic hierarchy process (AHP) 83–86
Dávila, G. A. 50
decent work and economic growth (SDG-8) 107
decision making 83, 105
decision-making **109**; centralization 50; Chinese workers 67; complex 83; I4.0 technologies 106, **109**; knowledge role in 22
Delbridge, R. 50
developing countries 105; *see also* countries
Devinatz, V. 30
dialogues 20, 22, 50–51, 64, 67, 73, 77, 78, 86, 89–90, 92, 96, 100, 102, 108
digital transformation 26, 31, 107–108, 110
dimension 83; cultural values 32, 44; horizontal/vertical 45; humane orientation 69; individualism/collectivism 45; knowledge and production 31; production management models 27; SECI model 26; social 27, 82; technical 27, 82
Ding, G. 25

Easterby-Smith, M. 8, 20
economic development: of Brazil 6–14; of China 1 6, 126–127, 129
economic interdependence 15
EIG Global Partners 9
Embraer 1
emerging markets 41, 109

employment 109–110; in Brazil and China 11–14, *14*, 88; for government and unions 63; job security and 68, 74; opportunities for Chinese workers 64
employment, economic growth (SDG-8) 110
Environmental, Health and Safety (EHS) 101
episteme 21; *see also* knowledge
epistemic/creative knowing **23**
epistemology 20
equitable and quality education (SDG-4) 110
Erden, Z. 22
error proofing **28**, 96, 100–101
explicit knowledge 14, 21, 23–25, 27, 29, 31, 33, 46, 82, 96, 110
externalization 26, 27, 45, 83, 85, 86, 96–98, 104

face 32, 41–43, 89, 93, 102; gaining 42, 74, 79; GE Hydro 63–64; losing 41–42, 69, 88–89, 93, 101–102; Maxion Wheels 69; opportunities and challenges in Brazil and China 11; saving 42–43, 74, 79, 104; Toyota Motor Corporation 74–75
face-prone people 41–42
factors 9–10, *85*; analytic hierarchy process (AHP) 82; cultural 32; enabling **95**, 101; external environment 26; knowledge management 25; knowledge-related 29; knowledge sharing 16, 21, *84*; negative 10; people 28–29; personal 26; process 27–28, **28**, 83; technological 26; work organization 26
Faucher, J. P. L 21
favouritism 50, 62
flexibility 30, 48, 108–109, **109**, 125, 129
Forbes Global 2000 11
foreign direct investments (FDIs) 1, **127**; inward 1, 3–5, **4**, **8**, 8–10, **10**; outward 1–3, **2–3**, 6–8, 7, **10**
formalism 48, 49–50, 51–52
Frank, A. G. 26

GAC Toyota Motor Co Ltd (GTMC) 71
GE Hydro 58–65, 94–101, **95**; authority 60–61; face 63–64; *guanxi* 62; humane orientation 65; job security 62–63; manufacturing lines 60; performance orientation 64; transparency 64
Germany 4, 9, 14, 46, 48, 105–106, 121–122, 127
Ghoshal, S. 16
Glisby, M. 33, 51, 105
global value chain 3, 123
governmental bureaucracy 50
guanxi 17, 43–44; directional 44; GE Hydro 62; Maxion Wheels 68; orientation 48; Toyota Motor Corporation 73–74
Gupta, V. 26

Hazlett, S. A. 21
Hecklau, F. 108
hierarchical management 49
hierarchical structure 60, 61
hierarchy 25, 50; for decision-making 67; in disciplined way 70; factors supporting knowledge sharing *84*; labour characteristics 78
Hildreth, P. M. 24
Hofstede, G. 32, 51
Holden, N. 31–33, 51, 105
House, R. J. 45, 64–65
Huawei 1
humane orientation: GE Hydro 65; Maxion Wheels 69–71; Toyota Motor Corporation 76–78
human resources 9, 66, 107, 122–124, 129
human resources management (HRM) 108
Hutchings, K. 32, 44, 45
hydraulic turbines 59
hydro-electric power station 59
Hygo Energy Transition and Golar LNG 9

implications 31, 43, 104–105
implicit knowledge 24–25, 32
incentives 29, 86, 98, 100–102; for Brazilians 75; employee satisfaction 77; financial 78–79, 99; individualism or collectivism 45; job satisfaction 30; knowledge generation/sharing 32, 96; for workers 30; workers motivation 70
inclusive, sustainable industrialization and promoting innovation (SDG-9) 110
incomplete pairwise comparison (IPC-AHP) 82–83, **84**
indigenous context 48
individualism/collectivism 32, 44–46, 49, 70, 75
Industrial environment 70, 82
Industry 4.0 (I4.0) 105–107, **106**; implementation 108; soft skills required for **109**

informal agreements 61
innovation 21, 23; holistic strategy 66; incremental 20, 24; internal learning processes and accumulated skills 24; technological development and 123; workers knowledge 20
internal communication application (ICA) 90
internalization 32, 86, 96–102, 104; Chinese workers preference 81; externalization and 45, 83; Maxion China 86
International Monetary Funds (IMF) 6
International Labour Organization (ILO) 14
inter-organizational ties 44
interpersonal relationships 15, 43, 49, 63, 73, 92, **109**
intra-organizational ties 44
inward (IFDIs) 1; Brazil **8**, 8–10, **10**; China 3–5, **4**
Ipe, M. 32, 51, 107
ISO 9000 89
Itau Unibanco 1

Japan 4, 47–48, 71, 74, 75
jeitinho 17, 48–49, 51–52, 63
job insecurity 32, 124
job satisfaction 25–26, 30, 46
job security: GE Hydro 62–63; Maxion Wheels 68; Toyota Motor Corporation 74
joint venture 66, 71, 126

kaizen 21, 50, 75, 94
Kimble, C. 24
KM-related research 110
know how 15, 21, 89, 107
knowing: in action 22, **23**; creative **23**; professional **23**; task **23**; virtual **23**
knowledge 20–23; acquisition 47, 108; characteristics **24**; context-free 21; contextual 50; conversion 14, 25–27, 29, 31, 33, 83–89, 111; defined 20; exchange 47; explicit 14, 21, 23–25, 27, 29, 31, 33, 46, 82, 96, 110; implicit 24–25, 32; local 32; perspectives **24**; as third dimension 27; types of 21; universal 21; workers 20–21, 82, 101, 111; *see also* tacit knowledge
knowledge-based integrated production management model *27*
knowledge management (KM) 20–33; in blue-collar workers 29–31; classification of 21–22; in cross-cultural contexts 31–33; described 23–29; and I4.0 110; influenced by 25; and its paradigms *21*; knowing in action **23**; particularistic approach 33, 105, 109
knowledge sharing 21, 25, 30, 42, 81–102; analytic hierarchy process (AHP) 82–86; attitude 45; barriers 26, 82, 105; blue-collar workers 15, 82–83; Brazil 47–52; China 41–52; context 50–51, 84; cross-cultural 33; culture 26, 110; openness in 32; research findings 86–101; tacit knowledge 33
Kuhn, T. S. 21

labor rights 63
leadership 14, 25, 49–50, 67, 108, **109**
lean 60, 94; manufacturing 28; thinking 20
learning 14–16, 28, 96; barriers 58; human 20; Industry 4.0 108; internal 24; machine 20; opportunities 107; organizational 25; processes 24
Lee, H. 25
logical inferences 20
loyalty 45, 50, 62
Luxembourg 9

macroeconomic conditions 11, 70
Made in China 2025 121, 127
Maxion Wheels 66–71; authority 67; face 69; *guanxi* 68; humane orientation 69–71; job security 68; performance orientation 69–71; transparency 69
meritocracy 78; among workers 99; competitiveness and 100
mianzi 90
multinational corporations (MNCs) 1, 15, 105, 108; in Brazil 16, 104; in China 16, 104; learning-related barriers 58
multinationals 41, 109; Brazilian 7
multiple-criteria decision-making (MCDM) 82–83; *see also* analytic hierarchy process
multi-skilled workers 30; *see also* workers
Muniz, J. 50, 82, 104
mutual understanding 16

Nakano, D. 24
Nascimento, L. O. 108
national contexts 1, 15, 105; *see also* context
national culture 31–32, 41; *see also* culture
The Netherlands 4, 6, 9
Nonaka, I. 21, 24, 25–27, 29

objectives 21, 26, 28–29, 51, 72–73, 83, 86
observation 20, 50
operators 22, 27–28, 31, 90–91, 94, 107; Brazilian 79; experienced 30, 90, 92, 94; incentive for motivating shop floor 29, 30; non-skilled 81; novice 25, 30, 96; skilled 81; socialization 85, 89; training offered by production leaders 92
organizational learning 25
orientation 41–42; feminine value 51; *guanxi* 48; humane 64–65, 69–71, 76–78; performance 64–65, 69–71, 76–78; relational 49
outward FDIs (OFDIs) 1; Brazil 6–8, 7, **10**; China 1–3, **2–3**

Pacific coexistence **109**
paradigms 107, 126; computational 21; of knowledge management *21*; organic 22; scientific 21
participation 6–8, 20, 110, 124
particularistic approach 33, 41, 81, 105, 109
Partnerships and Means of Implementation (SDG-17) 107–108
paternalistic leadership style 50
people 14–15, 22, 72, 74, 83, 101; assemblages of 22; behaviours 32; business 51; collaboration and synergy of 30; collectivistic culture positive impact on 45; face-prone 41–42; factors 28, 29; influence of experienced 25; integration of 31; migration of working 128; power distance 33; sense of worth 77
people-based (management) 22
people-based aspects 110
performance orientation: GE Hydro 64; Maxion Wheels 69–71; Toyota Motor Corporation 76–78; *see also* orientation
personal benefits 49
personalism 48, 50–52
personal relationship 30, 48, 50, 83, 92
perspective: blue-collar employee **25**; cognitive 24, **24**; constructivist **24**; of knowledge **24**; managerial 15, 33, 81, 98; of workers 98, 110
Petrobas 1
phronesis 21, 22; *see also* knowledge
poke yoke 28
Polanyi, M. 24, 96
Poleacovschi, C. 25, 78
Portuguese-speaking countries **5**, 5–6
power distance 33, 51
prescribed norms 50
Prinz, C. 108
problem-solving methods 21, 27, **28**, 83, 86, 90, 93–94, 96, 100–101
problem-solving strategy 48–49
process 11, 14–16; continuous improvement 50; factors 27, **28**, 101; internal learning 24; knowledge conversion 89; knowledge sharing 25, 33, 43, 96; manufacturing 109; operational 66; planning 110; production 30, 93, 107; productive 31; SECI knowledge 27; at shop floor 20
production management 25, 31; models 21, 27, *27*, 82
production routines 21
production system 20, 30, 48, 59, 94, 108
professional career development 49, 73
professional knowing **23**
public recognition 65, 71, 75

quality education (SDG-4) 107
quick changeover 28, **28**, 94, 96, 98, 100–101

reading 20, 83, 88, 98
reciprocity **23**, 48–49, 62
recognition 33, 41–42; based on knowledge 69; between Brazil and China 65; financial in Brazil 76; public 75
resistance 30
rewards 25, 26, 64–65, 69, 78–79, 92; extrinsic 42
Ribeiro, V. B. 110
Roberts, J. 22
rotor poles 60

5S **28**
Saaty, T. L. 84
Scherer, A. G. 21
Schwartz, S. 32
SECI model 26–27, 29; combination 26–27, 52, 104; externalization 26, 27, 45, 83, 85, 86, 96–98, 104; internalization 32, 45, 81, 83, 86, 96–102, 104; socialization 22, 26–27, 32, 50–51, 70, 83, 85–86, 89–90, 94, 97–102, 104
seiketsu **28**
seiri **28**
seiso **28**
seiton **28**
self-esteem 43
self-worth 25, 42, 74, 77

semi-automatic assembly lines 82
shared interpretations 16
shitsuke **28**
shop floor 15, 20–21, 24, 26–27, 29, 31–33, 50, 59, 66–68, 81–82, 84, 91, 92, 94, 97–98
Sié, L. 108
single-minute exchange of dies (SMED) 28
skills 14–15, 21, 24, 26, 29–30, 47, 72, 81, 96, 106–108, **109**, 124, 129
Snell, R. 33
social constructivism 20
social interactions **23**, 29, 30, 42–43, 47–48, 63, 73
socialization 22, 26–27, 32, 50–51, 70, 83, 85–86, 89–90, 94, 97–102, 104
social practice 25, 48
soft skills 107–108, **109**, 124
Spain 9
Spender, J. C. 21
standard operating procedures (SOPs) **28**, 83, 85, 88, 96
stator core laminations 60
stator winding bars/coils 60
strategy 41–42, 48–49, 66, 72, 108, 125, 127–128, 130
structure 28–29, 58–61, 66–67, 83, 93, 98
supervisors 24, 29, 66, 68, 72
Swidler, A. 32
synchronous electric generators 58–60, *59*, 84
synergy 21, 30

tacit-explicit knowledge 26–27, 33, 110
tacit knowledge 20, 23, 25, 31; characteristics of 22; conceptual foundation 24; defined 22; in Industry 4.0 108; quality of group 22; workers 60
Taylorism 20
team-oriented 47, 49
teamwork 29, 47, 74, 96, 101
techne 21; *see also* knowledge
technical orientation *see* orientation
technological factors 26
technology-based (information systems) 21
technology-based research 110
Thomas, A. 26
ties **23**, 63; inter-organizational 44; intra-organizational 44
Toyota Motor Corporation 71–78; authority 72–73; face 74–75; *guanxi* 73–74; humane orientation 76–78; job security 74; performance orientation 76–78; transparency 75–76
Toyota production system 20
training 14, 21–22, 84, 124, 129; formal 72, 96; and incentives 29; manufacturing 100; of new workers 30; shop floor 92; strategies 108
transgressive practice 49
transparency: GE Hydro 64; Maxion Wheels 69; Toyota Motor Corporation 75–76
trust, interpersonal 46–47

Uhlemann, T. H. J. 108
Ullah, A. S. 20
unions 63–64, 70, 74, 77, 79
United States 4, 9, 14, 44, 46, 121–122, 127
UN Sustainable Development Goals (SDGs) 107, 125

Vale 1
varieties of knowing in action **23**
Vertical Kaplan turbine 59, *59*
virtual knowing **23**
Von Krogh, G. 24

wisdom (phronesis) 21, 22, 50
workers 14; automotive 32; autonomy 30; blue-collar 15, 26, 29–31, 33, 50; Chinese and Brazilian 51, 60–62, 65, 67, 73–75, 98; collective sense-making and synergy among 21; cultural differences 96; engagement 110; knowledge sharing among 21; multi-skilled 30; production 15; skilled 107, 129; tacit knowledge 20, 60
work organizations 20, 24, 26, 27, 48
World Bank 9
World Investment Reports 9
World Trade Organizations 1

Xiaomi 1

Yakhlef, A. 108

For Product Safety Concerns and Information please contact our EU representative GPSR@taylorandfrancis.com
Taylor & Francis Verlag GmbH, Kaufingerstraße 24, 80331 München, Germany

www.ingramcontent.com/pod-product-compliance
Lightning Source LLC
LaVergne TN
LVHW021131300926
849160LV00010B/958

* 9 7 8 0 3 6 7 6 3 0 9 9 7 *